To

Happy wild gardening adventures!

Gary Thompson

Rewilding an Urban Garden

An Illustrated Diary of Nature's Year

Gerry Maguire Thompson

urbanwildgarden.com

Illustrations by Gerry and Marina

Rewilding an urban garden: An Illustrated Diary of Nature's Year

Published by WildBooks
Chez di Nook, 57 Connaught Avenue, BN43 5WL
September 2023

ISBN: 978-0-9559837-2-6

What readers are saying:

"Lovely book.... I really enjoyed it, and liked the quirky humour. Humour is something which is sometimes lacking in books about nature"

- Neil Ansell, author of *Deep Country, The Last Wilderness* and other classic wildlife books

"My missus loves your wonderful book, Gerry, couldn't put it down. Her mum had been really poorly for her last few months with us; so the missus would sit for hours just reading it to her; that will have such wonderful memories for her."

- Phil M

"I warmly recommend you read this book and let yourself be carried away by the beauty of the small, anecdotal stories about everything that comes to live in a small city garden. Thank you, Gerry."

- Magnus Sylvén: Co-director, Global Rewilding Alliance

"Wild gardening is a most grounding spiritual practice that boosts your physical health and mental well-being; we are co-creating with the universe. This wonderful and beautiful book, full of enchanting storytelling, quirky humour and wonderful tips, helps you to rewild your garden and your life."

- Robert Holden, author of *Higher Purpose* and *Happiness NOW!*

"A unique and beautifully observed book. Gerry has a wonderful gift in cooperation with the natural world and brings passion and presence to his writing."

- Malcolm Stern, Co-founder of Alternatives, psychotherapist and author

"Gerry is the Bill Bryson of wildlife gardening"

- Andy Mindel, founder and CEO of Wordtracker and Webventurer

Gerry Maguire Thompson is an Irish author of serious and humorous books, a rewilder and mentor to other writers. He also offers consultation services to wild gardeners and is available to give talks on the subject.

Gerry has had a passion for nature, wildlife and words since childhood.

urbanwildgarden.com
gerrymaguirethompson.com

To my much loved father Rev George Thompson, who instilled in me a love of the wild and the outdoors.

"We watch wild creatures because of what they tell us about ourselves, and about our sense of what it means to be wild and free."

Neill Ansell, Deep Country

Contents

Introduction.......01

January.......02
February.......32
March.......52
April.......72
May.......100
June.......122
July.......138
August.......160
September.......176
October.......194
November.......212
December.......226

The power of wild urban gardening.......240
Creating your own urban wildlife garden.......243
10 Steps you can take.......245
Bibliography and online resources.......250

"There are some who can live without wild things, and some who cannot."

Aldo Leopold: A Sand County Almanac 1949

Introduction

This is the story of our small wildlife garden in the city, told over nature's calendar year, sometimes with a touch of humour, and accompanied by drawn illustrations of the garden's wild denizens.

Every day in the garden brings new insights, surprises and drama as we get to know the wild creatures ever more intimately, learn how nature works in all its wondrous intricacy, and discover our deep connectedness with it all. The journey brings a great deal of fulfilment, joy and comfort in these often challenging times. It's amazing how many different life forms can be attracted into even a small urban outdoor space.

Creating your own wild garden brings great benefits to yourself, to your local wildlife, to your wider urban environment and even to the planet. It's mostly getting out of nature's way and letting her do her important work, with just a few interventions.

Thanks for joining me on this journey.

January

Jan 1st

Serious garden-watching resumes today after cessation of seasonal festivities. The resident male blackbird is stabbing at windfall fruit from the apple tree, still remaining intact on the ground through the winter. He's starting to look glossy and his beak is turning a brighter colour: preparing to defend this very desirable territory.

Jan 3rd

The sparrows are out in force today, with more fine weather after rain yesterday. I never tire of watching sparrows in the garden.

There's a large and growing flock who seem to never leave the garden. All their needs are met here: food, protection, nest-sites, safe roosting – and lots of opportunities to bicker at one another.

Over a couple of years the noise they make has stepped up as the size of the flock has steadily increased. It sounds cheerful to us, but it's mostly bickering. Their chatter is loudest when it's safest to do so, which is when they're ensconced in dense foliage; attracting attention when you're out in the open is dangerous. Even today, in mid-winter, I see passers-by stop and wonder about the cheerful sounding din coming out of the bushes. As people have increasingly noticed this sound and taken an interest, overheard mutterings have gradually changed from "Why is that garden such a mess/ why don't they cut their hedge/ what a jungle/ it's an absolute disgrace/ haven't these people heard of the lawnmower?" to "There's a lot more birds in this garden than ours/ it's a jungle – wonderful/ how can we make our garden more like that?" A lot of this attention can be credited to the sparrows because they're so noisy, so evident and so engaging.

Watching sparrows is not about waiting for something dramatic or spectacular to take place, though this occasionally happens. To me it's about entering their world, learning about them and connecting with the intricacies of their lives. They're engaging creatures, tolerant of human closeness; they draw you into their world. House Sparrows have evolved and adapted to living around humans. There's a colony which lives entirely indoors at London Heathrow Airport terminal; they nest behind lighting fittings and feed on crumbs on the floor at the food outlets. Sparrows have also bred 600 metres below ground in a working mine at Frickley Colliery in Yorkshire. Two birds, a male and female, entered the mine in 1975, followed by a third, and the current population grew from there. They're given food and water by the miners.

I shouldn't really have favourite species, but the sparrows are the ones I'd miss most if they weren't around. They're here within the garden all the time: they eat here, sleep here, breed and bring up their young here – all up close and within sight. They represent the most constant and most dynamic element of the whole little garden ecosystem. Of any species, they bring the most life to the scene for the greatest amount of the time; their presence and success provides an indication that the garden is working well.

Jan 5th

A woodmouse (*Apodemus Sylvaticus*: 'one who goes abroad among the sylvan glades') has been popping into the conservatory on the odd sunny day when we have the doors open, looking for something to eat. It's a creature with an undeniably high cuteness quotient: beautiful golden brown colouring, big eyes and ears, a long tail– and lacking the grey house-mouse's less endearing habit of moving permanently into your home. It's not nationally rare, but found more often in rural rather than urban settings like ours so it's an exciting presence here. The large eyes and ears are there because it's usually nocturnal – mainly to avoid daytime predators – but is flexible about working hours in winter when its reserves of stored food may have run out – and especially ready to make an exception when crumbs from home-made organic scones and shortbread are available, as is the case with our conservatory cream tea today.

The woodmouse is primarily a seed eater; I watched one last autumn running to and fro for hours between the ground under the birds' seed feeder and the log pile where it had set up a storage facility. They also eat snails and insects in spring. They don't really hibernate, but go in and out of a torpid state when the weather is warmer or when hunger strikes. The big enemy in urban settings, of course, is the domestic cat.

This little creature tends to pop in once each day for a couple of days, and is surprisingly undaunted by our presence. It's quite happy to move around my feet, picking up whatever bits fell from my plate, as long as I don't move suddenly.

Jan 6th

I love watching the wildlife from inside the house. I glance out often, plus I have several periods in the day set aside for a prolonged look. Staring out the window while wondering what to write is part of the writer's job description. I used to watch daytime TV during work breaks, but live wildlife watching is superior. It has drama, mystery, soap opera, tragedy and comedy– and that's just the sparrows. There's always something happening. There's rich life out there and you see everything in close-up detail, with the leading characters undisturbed by your presence.

There is immense joy in this connexion with the inhabitants of our little wildlife haven and the intimate insights into their lives. Most days there isn't anything rare or exotic to look at; much of it may seem mundane or commonplace, but when you're immersed over a period you see all kinds of subtle stuff going on. I hope this will come across in these daily observations.

Jan 7th

The blackbird is now systematically eating ivy berries all day long. Blackbirds seem to use this strategy throughout the year: focus on one type of fruit at a time and guard it against other takers until it's all gone, then move on to another type. Ivy is reliable food for them in the depths of winter. Nobody else outside the thrush family (to which the blackbird belongs) seems to be able to stomach these nutritious but bitter tasting berries which contain nearly as many calories by weight as a Mars bar. Or maybe the blackbird is successfully chasing everyone else away from them rather than eating them now.

Jan 9th

In the late afternoon I notice numbers of redwing gathering in the big ash tree just outside our garden gate; as the sun goes down more and more of them congregate until there are well over a hundred.

The redwing is an attractive bird: not actually having red wings but instead a bold red marking beneath the wing: pedantically speaking it should be called *redarmpit*. Like another winter visitor we see here, the fieldfare, it's a Scandinavian member of the thrush family which flies to climes such as ours when the weather gets colder and food is scarce in the homeland. They travel round the country in large flocks looking for food hoards like the holly berries in our garden. When they find one, they guard it to prevent other birds taking any, and spend a few days' resting from their journey knowing they will be able to refuel just before leaving for their next pit-stop. They often fly at night and their high-pitched cheeping call can often be heard as they pass overhead in their large flocks. At the end of winter they return home to breed.

Jan 10th

The redwings are still gathered in the ash tree in huge numbers, now covering its whole canopy.

Jan 11th

I look out first thing in the morning to check on the redwings: they've gone. And so has every berry that was on every holly tree in the garden. They probably departed in the middle of the night.

Jan 13th

A cold, bright day: perfect for the main annual prune. Most things in the garden are left for nature to take its course; we've allowed our surrounding hedge to grow up and enclose the space, but every year or so we need to bring down the tops of the shrubs and trees and cut back where they grow too far into the central open area. The ideal is to create dappled shade but this would quickly turn into primordial jungle if left completely alone.

Everything grows like mad in this garden even though there's a lot of shade; it's become an extremely fertile ecosystem. Encouraging dense hedge growth around the perimeter with a central open space simulates a woodland clearing, or you could say woodland edge turned inside out; in nature woodland edge is an exceptionally rich and biodiverse ecological niche. For 99% of human history we have lived in and around woodland, so it's also good to have it on our doorstep where we can indulge in a spot of our own shinrin-yoku or Japanese style forest bathing.

Even when we became farmers 11,000 years ago woodlands and forests were still part of our everyday lives.

We have had a policy of encouraging or introducing native shrubs and small trees and then coaxing native climbers like honeysuckle or ivy to form a dense canopy through and over them, and this is paying off. The system brings the triple benefit to small birds of providing well hidden nesting sites, cosy overnight roosting out of the wind and rain, and protective cover to dive into when predators appear – which they do. It also provides shelter for invertebrates through the winter – a food source for the birds in times of scarcity – and opportunity for mammals like mice and squirrels to get around the garden without being vulnerable. Deciduous trees on their own, having dropped their leaves in winter, do not provide this range of benefits.

This pruning raises the question: how to use the resultant cuttings within the garden ecosystem, one of our guiding principles? I have a cunning plan: I push them down into the lower reaches of the hedge, where the foliage is thinner, so a dense hedgerow bottom grows up, interwoven with ivy and other creepers. Birds like wrens and robins love this low cover, as do small mammals.

Honeysuckle growing up through hawthorn is the classic combination of tree and creeper for diverse wildlife. Honeysuckle is very fast growing, likes to make a canopy of leaves on the outside of the tree it's on, and is pretty much evergreen throughout winter. Ivy is good too, though not so quick growing – completely evergreen and one of the best native plants for wildlife. It offers nectar and pollen for insects in autumn when not much else is flowering, and those dark berries that last through the winter – with an especially high fat content– are crucial food sources for some birds. Ivy supports around fifty species, perhaps second only to the oak in this regard. There's a widely held view that ivy strangles and takes nutrients from its host tree, but this is untrue; indeed ivy often holds up trees that have died, thus providing valuable aerial dead wood sources for insects and birds that prey on them, or nesting opportunities within the cavities.

Holly is another outstanding mainstay of this 'jungle-hedge' – fast growing and providing dense protective cover with copious amounts of flowers and then berries. The height and density of this wall of prickly vegetation makes it difficult for predator birds to see in.

With the high surrounding super-hedge, the only place where passers-by can see into the garden is at the narrow gateway which is arched over with foliage and obscured from the street - it's a place of mystery in stark contrast to many nearby gardens that are wildlife deserts with manicured lawns, bare-earth flowerbeds and hardstandings for multiple vehicles. This makes people exceedingly curious. We see them glance in as they pass by, then come back for a closer look. "You've got another world in there", passers by have said, and "It's a secret magical garden!" Children are especially spellbound by its allure, so the garden is providing an element of nature education. Every dog that passes the gateway stops, looks in, smells wildness and wants to linger. It is, as they're all noticing, a different world in a garden, a complete mini-ecosystem in itself.

A lot of people think that rewilding your garden is an all-or-nothing thing: that you have to rewild completely or not at all. But not so - for many people a hybrid cultivated/wilded space will be ideal. And for others just letting part of a lawn go its own natural way is enough.

Jan 15th

Haven't seen so many of the sparrows for a day or two – perhaps due to the pruning – but this reminds me of something I've been pondering for a while. Having this garden has led me to wonder more about the amazing workings of nature and try to get answers to the questions that have been puzzling me. I'm a very puzzled person. Today I'm dwelling on the question of where all the dead birds go. Why do we see so few of them? Most small birds like sparrows, bluetits or robins don't live very long. Obviously a certain number get caught and eaten by sparrow-hawks, crows, magpies and the like, and the younger and older ones may be more prone to this fate. Some may die in their nests, and the bodies remain there till found by a scavenger. Some become roadkill. Some will be killed by cats.

But a great number must die while roosting under cover at night - especially when the weather is bitterly cold and food scarce - and fall off their perch; winter is the time of greatest risk of mortality for all bird species. So why aren't there little bodies lying in the bottom of the hedges in my garden, below these very popular roosting places? I know there aren't serious numbers of ground scavengers going in there, so there should be a certain number of tiny corpses or skeletons, yet I've never seen any– and I'm somewhat obsessive about these things. Some small mammals and even insects dig the bodies of deceased small birds into leaf mould and into the ground, to eat at their leisure, but I think I'd have seen this if it was happening here. The numbers just don't tally.

Have a think about it. Say you have two robins in your garden for a breeding season. Those two birds could have two broods of five young each, creating up to ten young robins. But you're not seeing twelve robins in your garden, or even seven robins – you're only seeing two, and then maybe only one when breeding's over. So how many robins have died in one year? Research has shown that about 60% of adult robins die each year, and the average life expectancy of the robin is 1.1 to 1.2 years. The oldest known robin lived to eight and a half years, but that was completely exceptional. A bluetit has lived to 21 years – probably missing family members it survived for the latter 20 of those years. That's equivalent to a human living to 800 years of age. Awful.

So among small birds in general, about half the adult birds and the great majority of the infant birds I see in my garden will be dead by the time this diary gets to December. This seems drastic, but it enables populations to remain roughly constant. Even a small improvement on this year-on-year enables steady population growth. And steady growth, year on year, is what we're seeing in our garden's population of sparrows, blackbirds and other species. So our fortunate birds are beating the average figures, which is excellent at a time when populations are declining across the board nationally.

The mystery remains, though – there are still a lot of them dying but unaccounted for. Maybe the missing sparrows disappear into another dimension: a sort of sparrallel universe perchance?

Jan 16th

Heard from next-door neighbour that the local sparrow-hawk had been sitting in her garden a few days ago – that may well be the main reason for the sparrows keeping a low profile recently.

Jan 17th

In the afternoon I'm sitting in the garden, just quietly observing; it becomes a kind of meditation. For a while it may seem like nothing is happening; but really there is never nothing happening at any season of the year or time of day. It might be slow, it might be subtle, but something will be going on. There'll be an animal or a bird or an insect doing something – today's it's a bumble bee queen - or a new plant that you hadn't noticed before. And there'll be sound - birdcalls, occasional buzz of an insect, a fox's shriek in the late evening – and the longer you listen, the more layers of sound you realise there are. The intricate web of nature is always there and is always amazing in its workings.

Observing this challenges one's habitual evaluation of what is significant and worthy of attention. I realise more and more that the everyday and the mundane are in fact extraordinary: the amazingness of the commonplace. The seemingly prosaic or unglamorous species like the sparrow or the earthworm or the dandelion can reveal itself as extraordinary and charismatic when we give it our full attention. It makes you question the whole concept of what is conventionally appealing, which is no bad thing in this age of the tyranny of stereotypical celebrity based allure. And of course it applies equally to the human species; haven't you noticed that the most seemingly uninteresting individual becomes fascinating when they reveal themselves, who they are and what makes them tick?

So there's always some of the obvious stuff I can see and hear – like the trees, the plants and the more common birds - and then there's stuff that I can't see or hear but know is there. I know, for instance that there are more birds than I can immediately see, hidden in the shrubbery. I know that there are large numbers of invertebrates over-wintering in the ivy. And I know there's plenty more going on at levels down to microscopic entities like fungal microbes and bacteria. It's a continuum, an infinite depth of detail that signifies ever deepening levels of the overall interconnected web of which this little garden is part, of which I am part. It's possible to see our personal interconnexion with all these diverse elements of a garden as a microcosm of our place on the planet and in the universe. One of the basic discoveries of quantum physics is that at the subatomic level no particles exist except in relationship to others.

Connecting everyday with wildlife in the garden – even in the city – takes us to our deeply embedded way of being: integration with our wild natural environment. If there was a twenty-four hour clock which timed our evolution from being creatures crawling out of the primordial soup up to where we are now, our modern detached-from-nature way of living in houses and cities would be a fraction of a second before midnight. This is why nature writing has had such a resurgence in recent years. But interest in nature and wildness is not some passing, exotic hobby: it's our deepest level of being. It's where we're coming from, and where we still belong, and where we still need to be able to be. That's why, I believe, having a wildlife garden can provide such profound and diverse benefits to all aspects of our wellbeing: physical, mental, emotional, spiritual and social.

Realising this interconnectedness, it's beginning to dawn on at least some of us that humanity's health and future depends on the fate of all the plant and animal species on the planet, down to the tiniest speck. We need to develop what nature writer Mark Cocker calls "a reawakened reverence for life beyond our own species" (see bibliography) and a widespread surge in wildlife gardening could really help with that.

Sensing all this, for this moment of time I suddenly feel that transcendent momentary sense that nothing needs to be changed to make anything any better. This is the Tao of wild gardening.

When this ecological richness and diversity develops in your garden, you know you're doing something right in your role of custodian and maintainer. There's a satisfying sense that you're moving at least this little patch and its surroundings in the right direction; you're playing some small part in the effort to alter humankind's deep seated habit of ecological destruction.

Jan 18th

The bee that's around at the moment is the Buff-tailed Bumblebee, *Bombus Terrestris*, often the earliest bee to be seen out and about. It nests underground, ideally in old mouse burrows.

I've been watching the sparrows feeding today: it's mysterious. They often leave a full feeder for hours, while at other times they pounce on it as soon as you put it out. I suppose it could often be about the availability of other food sources, but at this time of year there isn't an excess of other food around.

What I've observed is that sparrows do have an identifiable breakfast time and dinner time. Why would they have this pattern when food is available at other times of day? Many other species, such as our goldfinches, eat opportunistically anytime they can find food. The conclusion I've come to is that it's all about the intricacies of their metabolism.

Here's what the sparrow day looks like. After a lengthy period waking up and chattering in their roosting tree, they move up to its top twigs to warm up in any rays of sunshine available, even if there isn't a great deal of heat in them. Then it's time for their morning meal, which serves to recover from hunger developed overnight and to provide energy for the day. Then the flock just does low-grade foraging.

The next big feeding occasion is their late afternoon meal, which serves to get them through the night. Small birds like sparrows can put on what is known as brown fat which is processed almost instantaneously, and is burned up quickly too. After this meal they try to catch the last of any rays available on the tops of their roosting tree, then move down into their roosting zone, where they chatter for another extended period before finally settling down as it gets dark. So eating a big meal in the late afternoon makes sense; the brown fat they put on needs to last them through the night, so there's no point in putting it on too early in the day. Likewise upon waking: the fat reserves are used up so they need a big meal then too.

This pattern is especially crucial in cold weather, but is a feature of their metabolism all the year round. Funnily enough, they never wake and start to eat immediately; they need to go through their ritualistic flock-affirming procedure of chattering and then warming themselves before thinking of food. Maybe their metabolism is at a low ebb after sleep and they need to get it going before handling digestion. So if a seed filler is refilled at the wrong time it will just be ignored, or exploited by other species. Recognising this 'brown fat' scenario, we put out fat blocks with insects in them during prolonged spells of severely cold weather. When this is available they will eat the suet and completely ignore any seed available. It's all about fat and weight gain.

Then of course there's the matter of all the other things they need to find time for in the day besides food intake. A lot of time is spent on reinforcing that social order. And depending on season, there will be pairing up, mating, nesting, looking after fledglings and then moulting before winter comes on again. It seems like they do a lot of stuff for fun, too – preening, chatting and listening to gossip, sunbathing, dust bathing, maybe power napping. They seem to enjoy squabbling and fighting a lot, year round, with everyone joining in; it's a popular sport. Having time for all this other stuff, rather than having to spend the whole day searching for food, is a luxury that flocking birds can afford; starlings and rooks have similar patterns of leisure and social activity. It's also a sign of a healthy colony in a favourable environment, which is reassuring.

If you do provide food for birds – especially in the winter – it's important to provide it consistently, as the birds will come to depend on this source being available as part of their overall food plan, and it will have become a key element in their survival.

Jan 19th

I regard our own family as part of this garden eco-system, interacting with the other wild characters; Rosa – our cocker spaniel - is a particularly active interactor. She's now getting on for fifteen years old – 105 in human years – but is still youthful, sprightly and mischievous. She takes a keen interest in anything she can see moving in the garden, though her eyesight isn't what it was. Like all spaniels, she exercises selective hearing when you're trying to get her to stop doing something she doesn't want to stop doing.

We don't let Rosa loose in the garden, but she still has an impact; we take her through on the lead several times a day on the way to her walks. Today she's particularly interested in a blackbird feeding on an apple; she stands stock still, rivetted. Her ancestral gun-dog genes are coming through; but she doesn't run at it – finally the training is starting to work, after fifteen years.

The blackbirds, sparrows and other birds are not much bothered by Rosa's presence, and carry on with whatever they're doing as long as she's not right on top of them. They seem to have learned that she isn't a threat; indeed, I think they understand that a garden where a dog makes regular appearances isn't going to be frequented by Public Enemy #1: the local cat; yes, I have a Public Enemy list.

Rosa has loved cats most of her life, wagging her tail when she saw one and approaching to make friends; then one day a cat turned and bolted, which seemed to re-set Rosa's feline reflex to the chase-and-try-to-kill manufacturer's default setting. This change was good news as far as I was concerned, as it makes cats all the more wary of entering the garden. I personally love cats, but as everyone knows they are prolific killers of wild life-forms right up to the size of a pheasant.

Jan 20th

Taking Rosa out for her bed-time walk and toiletries last night, I spotted a fox across the road. This was one I recognised, a big old dog fox with a woolly face that makes him look like a bear. I've seen him around here for a long time, and I know where he lives – under an unused shed at nearby allotments. He's wary of people and dogs, which is probably how he got to be big and old. Tonight as usual he keeps his distance, then moves away.

Jan 21st

The resident robin starts singing at night when I take Rosa out in the dark. If I shine my head-torch towards the tree where it roosts I can literally get it to start and stop by turning the torch on and off. Robins are known for singing when anything resembling dawn occurs – notably when urban street lights switch on for the night. Their song is automatically prompted by any light coming on with a level of 0.01 candlepower or more. That's not much.

I long wondered why birdsong should sound so great to us; I'm the kind of guy who wonders about things like that. The question I always want to ask in such cases is, what's the evolutionary benefit? Because benefit to practical survival is always there, and the behaviour of all species will always be motivated by the three main aims of getting enough to eat, not getting eaten, and making babies. So, what positive developmental advantage would we obtain through gradually evolving to find birdsong so mesmeric? Especially when for the birds themselves it's purely an expression of life-and-death struggle for survival and reproduction?

I can think of a number of possible answers. As an ancient species out in the wild without wristwatches and calendars, birdsong for us would be one useful indicator of time of day and of the progression of the seasons. It would also be an indicator of potential food opportunity– and of potential danger when alarm calls are sounded. Plentiful birdsong may also have indicated to us as nomadic hunters that we're in a wildlife-productive area that may make it worthwhile to hang around for a while. Birdsong in general is one of the strong sensory experiences that draws us into the world of nature and wildness to which we're still so primordially connected.

But there must be more to it than this – it doesn't really explain the auditory beauty aspect– and there is. Biologists at McGill University in Montreal have recently discovered that songbirds and humans have very similar biological hardwiring in the brain that shapes how we each produce and perceive sounds. Young birds, they've found, are intrinsically predisposed to learn certain particular kinds of sound pattern over others, and these favoured patterns happen to resemble those found most frequently in human speech and in human music too.

These common brain mechanisms or 'universals' had already been demonstrated by linguistic experts as occurring across all human languages. Naom Chomsky postulated that these constitute a 'universal grammar' which aids language learning in the individual as well as communication across language and cultural barriers. But the direct link to the same patterns in birdsong is new.

So when we listen to birdsong it isn't about aesthetics; we're connecting directly to the ancient common linguistic forms that our innate brain wiring recognises. The blackbird has been found to use 286 different notes, whereas the nightingale uses over 1000, with 250 different songs of extraordinary complexity. The more of these universal patterns a bird weaves into the song the more spellbound we become.

Jan 22nd

Two bluetits are forming a promising relationship, hopping round one another on the apple tree when the sparrows are not in evidence – they seem to keep away from those slightly bigger and definitely more assertive birds.

Having finished stuffing all those cuttings from the top pruning of the shrubs into gaps low in the hedges, I was delighted to see a wren systematically hopping through it all right at the bottom level. Early viewing for nest potential, or foraging for food?

Jan 23rd

The bluetits have never been interested in the seed feeder, but today I see them eating from it. Why? I finally work out the explanation: earlier this morning, while making porridge with a variety of seeds, I had spilled sunflower seeds on the floor at home. Not wanting to waste these, I had added them to the early morning fill of the seed feeder; the regular mix only includes sunflower seeds in their hulls.

The most surprising aspect is that the one morning the feeder contains something of special interest to them, the bluetits are on it like a shot. Mystery solved. They must be spending a lot of their time just watching from cover, waiting for special opportunities like this. It shows there's a lot going on in the garden that isn't immediately visible.

Jan 24th

Just spotted one of the bluetits looking into one of the old nest-boxes - in January! This must be how far ahead of breeding season these little birds plan their real estate deals.

I'm watching the sparrows as they finally settle down to roost in the holly tree as darkness falls. All has gone quiet. Then I notice one bird hop down to the lowest branch of the tree, do a poo, and hop back up to where it was before. Seems like this is sparrow etiquette: you just don't poo on someone else's head while they're asleep. We've all been there.

Jan 25th

It's particularly dark this evening, completely overcast. Taking Rosa out for her night-time outing, we encounter a different fox – a lot younger and sleeker than Big Old Bear Fox – and a lot less wary of people and dogs. It must have grown up close to people, as many urban fox youngsters do these days, perhaps born under a garden shed where the human family appreciates and maybe feeds them.

This fox seemed to be loitering right outside our garden gate, as if waiting for us, barely six feet away. I wonder if Big Old Bear Fox has been driven out of the territory – or may even be dead? The thought saddens me, even though he has probably already had an unusually long life; average life expectancy for foxes is under two years and he's well over that age.

Rosa is unaware of the fox; she's looking in a completely different direction. She detects foxes mostly by smell; once she does that, she lets out a single bark – it's her "there's-a-fox-nearby" signal. Then she will usually take off like a rocket, nose to the ground, zigzagging around to follow the scent wherever the fox has gone. But today she's just quietly looking into the distance.

Jan 26th

Today, as happens from time to time, I see the two carrion crows that are resident in our street, sitting in the big ash tree outside our garden gate, just checking things out. They never come into the garden, but I'm glad to see them there because they are arch-enemies of my arch-enemies the magpies, and fight with them for territory. I disapprove of the magpies' fledgling-marauding activities later in the year and I find their strident rachetty cries annoying.

Once in a while I want to watch something more epic or more exotic or more savage than what's happening in my garden: a cheetah making her first kill on the Serengeti, maybe; a two day old Barnacle Goose gosling making a terrifying leap off 300 foot high cliffs in Greenland and bouncing off rocks all the way down; or a giant crocodile leaping from the river to grab an unfortunate wildebeest by the head. At times like this I turn to nature telly, which is getting better all the time.

But why is it that David Attenborough is the only person whose commentary really works for TV nature documentaries? So many other series are ruined by the voice-overs, mainly provided by professional actors who feel they have to rack up the emotional component to an overly intense level. This isn't helped by scripts that big things up still further; in a typical non-DA nature programme, you'll hear a stream of over-egged descriptive clichés: ".. scenes of indescribable beauty stretch out in every direction in this vast and unspoilt wilderness..."; "...the young Ibex seems destined to be swept to its death in the raging torrent..."; "..the leopard family will certainly starve if this mother's hunt is not successful!" No pressure, then. I hate it.

Yet the surprising thing is that The Attenborough puts plenty of emotion into his commentary too, and lots of up-and-down cadence in his delivery; yet it totally works. Perhaps it's his genuine, deep-seated passion and caring that makes the difference, in contrast to the jobbing actors pulled in for voice-overs. And the more convincing these luvvies try to make their presentation, the less convincing it seems to be. Plus those over-the-top scripts...

Jan 27th

I'm delighted to hear – from the dog-walking fraternity, who spot more wildlife than everyone else in the street put together – that Big Old Bear Fox is still alive and still around. Maybe he's been pushed into an adjacent territory – or maybe he's being tolerated by New Young Fox – maybe as a relative? Maybe even as potential father to offspring?

Passing my neighbour's house in the morning, I hear a big din of sparrow chatter coming from a small holly bush in her garden. This is a new development. Unlike me, our neighbour prunes and shapes her holly bushes very closely, with the result that this one has grown a dense outer layer of overlapping prickly leaves, like armour plating. This has proved to be an equally ideal safety habitat for small birds. I've realised from this that our resident flock has been increasing so successfully that population overspill has spread to form new flocks in a number of gardens nearby, including our neighbour's. It's gratifying.

Last night I had a wildlife-related dream in which I learned that, as a little known part of their life cycle, herring are actually born in upstream rivers. At a certain stage in their development hundreds of thousands of these adolescent herrings, knowing they need to go down to the sea but not knowing how to get there, are greeted in the river by adult herring who have travelled upstream in vast shoals to meet them. The adults then guide the adolescents downstream in a very particular and beautiful way: it's done in pairs, each pair comprising a fully grown herring and a youngster, dancing upright together in the water until they reach the sea. Now that's something I'd like to see a nature documentary about - David?

Jan 28th

Today at 7.55am I watched the sparrow-hawk crash into the flock of sparrows as they were sunning themselves on top of the roosting tree, ahead of going about their day's business. The sparrows immediately dived back deep into cover and stayed there for quite a while. The attack was unsuccessful. Who needs big-game nature TV ? And how long do birds know to wait till it's safe to come out? Probably a balance between risk of predation and getting enough food to make it through the day, especially at this time of year. This attack reminds me that people who have good sparrow stocks available all day every day all year are in danger of setting up a snack bar for the hawks.

Big Old Bear Fox and New Young Fox have been seen – together! So now I'm wondering if they're a couple. Sentimentally, I hope this is so. I'd be delighted for Big Old Bear Fox to become a father once more...probably for the last time.

Jan 29th

A mild day. The pair of collared doves we see a lot have started their shows of affection in the garden. Maybe this means we're going to have an early spring. They often feed under the seed feeder when the sparrows have wreaked their havoc – provided the wood pigeon isn't around in which case it takes precedence.

The wood pigeons have already been mating noisily in the hazel tree – but that doesn't mean anything about weather expectations. They do it all year round – then build poorly constructed nests from which the eggs fall out, so they have to start mating all over again. The male doesn't seem to mind this extra duty one bit. Maybe that's his plan.

This evening I heard the first twilight mating-plus-territorial song of the year from the resident male blackbird: it's beautiful and uplifting as ever. This is perhaps these islands' most popular singing bird; it's very widespread and fits in well with many people's lives. I know this bird is probably saying, "This is my territory so don't even think about coming into my space or you'll seriously regret it" but I never fail to feel joy from hearing it, especially just before dawn and again at dusk. Who knows, perhaps the bird feels joy too: the joy of telling others to **** off? That's a sentiment I sometimes experience myself.

Breeding doesn't usually start till March at the earliest, yet holding onto this patch and attracting the attention of females is clearly already on this bird's mind. He knows there are rich pickings here with the windfall apples and berries from holly, ivy, pyracanthas and mahonia throughout the year, and plenty of worms and other invertebrates at ground level, plus dense foliage for well hidden nesting sites: a real estate feature which blackbirds are particular about. So he's already started up the process of telling females what a great place it would be for them to settle down with him, and telling males not to think of trying to muscle in.

I'm not alone in finding the dawn and dusk songs of the blackbird hauntingly beautiful. In some of the earliest writings we have from these islands, Irish monks of the Celtic Christian era wrote poems about the beauty that surrounded them, as they lived alone in their solitary cells on the Atlantic seaboard:

> "Sweet I think the blackbird's warbling;
> At its sound I fall asleep;
> The tunes I hear are music to my soul"
>
> - from Penguin Classics, *A Celtic Miscellany*

The weather turns colder again. At 8am the temperature is below freezing and two wood pigeons are courting on a horizontal branch at a distance from one another. The female flies over to the male who bows deeply to her, cooing away. She sidles up to him but he doesn't do anything else. She flies off to another male fifty metres away. He's immediately interested, but she flies straight back to the first male. He repeats his previous behaviour and still takes things no further. She decides to give up on it. They sit next to one another in the cold with their heads drawn down into their bodies and feathers fluffed up. His body language is 'I'd love to, but can we wait till it's warmer?' I've never seen a wood pigeon turn down an offer like this.

The pair of collared doves pause their infatuation and focus instead on eating seed under the feeder - doing it together. They do everything together, never more than a foot apart. It's rather endearing. My partner would hate it if I did that sort of carry-on with her.

Jan 30th

The freeze deepens; now the ground is covered in hoar frost. Looking out my upstairs window at dawn, I see a dead fox in our next door neighbour's garden, lying frozen and covered in white frost crystals. The neighbours let me into their garden. I'm pretty sure this is New Young Fox. She clearly didn't die of hunger, because she's in pristine condition – apart from being dead obviously.

I suspect poisoning. There are some vocal individuals locally who want all foxes dead – not because they have chickens, which would be understandable – but because they feel that nature must be controlled and wildness eradicated. I find this attitude disturbing to say the least. It seems to go along with needing hedges to be tidy, wanting grass verges cut back to the ground on a weekly basis, and turning front gardens into sterile hard standings – because untidiness is evil; weeds are evil; uncontrolled animal wildlife are clearly vermin and must be eradicated. To me, it's the same impulse that humanity has displayed for a very long time– to conquer wilderness and establish 'order'– which has played a big part in getting the state of the planet to where it is now.

Jan 31st

Heard this morning of two more fox deaths that occurred during last night in our part of town. Definitely poisoning, then – and systematic. I called our local wildlife police officer – and how great it is that we have one here – but he tells me that nothing much can be done. Poisoning is only illegal if the poison bait is put down where pets could eat it, such as a public park.

The sun is shining. In this hard frost at 7.45am the first male song-thrush of the year starts singing on the highest tip of the highest holly tree in the garden. It seems early in the year as well as in the day; there's clearly strong motivation for this strident song sequence even though breeding season is far off. The answer is probably the perceived threat to territory from those Viking birds, the redwings and fieldfares.

Perching on the highest viewpoint in the vicinity – as thrushes are wont to do– and singing your heart out is a high-risk strategy, and numbers of thrushes are taken this way every year by sparrow-hawks and other birds of prey.

Many people tell me they have difficulty identifying the calls of the song-thrush, because it contains so many variations and they're looking for a typical call. The key identification factor is that they can make just about every kind of sound, but each phrase will always be repeated between three and eight times. Sometimes you can hear two male thrushes competing to attract females; one will sing forth an eloquent stream of repeated phrases, then the other will exactly repeat this sequence as emphatically as it can; then the first will do another sequence, and so on.

Next time you pass a singing thrush, stop and listen. It's magical, endlessly inventive, and you can be spellbound for as long as it keeps singing. But don't look directly at it or it will stop, suddenly aware of its vulnerability to predation.

The sparrows are having their first splash of the year in the birdbath, always a joy to watch. They're so exuberant and noisy that I can't believe they're not having a terrific time. My beloved sparrows continue to be a key part of my emotional support system, so full of vitality and effervescent chattiness are they in any weather and any time of day. I love listening to them; they sound cheerful and optimistic to me, though I'm also perfectly aware that they're mostly bitching, arguing, fighting and complaining to one another. I don't care; cheerfulness, optimism and full-of-life-ness are still the effects their chatter has on me.

Anthropomorphic, moi? Yes.

February

Feb 1st

Many people in the northern hemisphere don't like February as it's usually the coldest winter month; winter's been going on for a while and they crave sunshine. I decided a long time ago that I cannot let my happiness depend on British weather. I love February.

I love hearing the piercing nocturnal noises the foxes make as the male follows the female around, trying to keep other males away, both partners being playful and often reverting to cub behaviour while courting and getting ready for sex. Bloodcurdling noises, playful behaviour, reverting to infant behaviour.... we've all been there.

Today the resident grey squirrel is looking for the hazelnuts she hid in the garden last autumn – but the ground is cold and hard. Contrary to common belief, squirrels don't hibernate, so they need to find food throughout winter.

This dedicated squirrel habit is the reason we get so very many hazel saplings sprouting up all over the garden in spring; the squirrels find enough to stay alive, but don't find them all. So this individual is acting as accidental nursery-woman, supplying us with extra hazel bushes to supply to other rewilding gardeners. Many other shrubs in the garden– like wild plum, hawthorn, honeysuckle, ivy, dog rose, wild cherry and holly– also reproduce themselves so prolifically in this fertile soil - protected by the high hedging - that there are plenty of seedlings and rooted suckers which are excessive to needs. They also need to be removed because they would fill up the central open space that's needed to maintain diversity of habitat.

So in the winter we dig these out, pot them up and grow them on as saplings for a season or two till they have a healthy root system and substantial size, then give them to neighbours or use them to re-wild open spaces or fill gaps in local wild hedges in the neighbourhood, with these all-native species and generally increase local biodiversity.

Feb 2nd

One of the great things about having a wildlife garden is that you keep getting new wild plants brought in as seeds, many of which are edible for humans. We're managing to find a variety of foragable plants to eat now even though it's still late winter: burdock roots, dandelion roots and leaves, plantain, sow thistle, hawthorn berries and a variety of leafy shoots. One of the great things about including wild plants in your diet is that they help you be in rhythm with whatever season you're in, because those plants are responding day-to-day to those changing conditions, and that's what you're eating.

Feb 3rd

The resident male blackbird, having finished off the ivy berries in the recent cold weather, has noticed a few well-hidden holly berries on the lower branches, missed by the Viking hordes of redwing last month.

Feb 4th

Very mild weather. A large bumble bee is visiting the flowers of the Mahonia Japonica for nectar. At this time of year it's got to be a queen– the only one who survives through the winter– needing some nourishment to get through the cold months. So on occasional warmer days like this she emerges and follows the exquisite scent to this flower. Also known as Oregon Grape, mahonia isn't native but is a valuable asset because it flowers at this time of year when little else does, then bears berries which the blackbirds adore in spring when fruit is also scarce.

Feb 5th

Noticed that I've left the tops of the holly trees still too tall after January's big prune, allowing for the rapid re-growth they will make this coming year. Took the tops down a couple of feet, which also makes them grow bushier lower down. I'd never realised before I started wilding this garden just how fast-growing hollies can be. This time I've invented a new technique to make the upper foliage more dense - as the tops are cut, instead of removing them I let them drop down into the body of the tree. Maximum foliage density is the number one criterion for bird roosting, nesting and protection from predators. I'm a bit obsessed with it.

Feb 6th

I might have done a bad thing cutting the holly tops back still lower than in January: it may have prompted a sparrow-hawk attack. The high foliage usually makes it difficult for predatory birds to see what's going on within the garden, and the

sparrows were used to having the hedge higher and perching in there.

The first thing I know about it is when I'm looking out from my upstairs office window and see the hawk crouching on the ground with a sparrow in its talons, spreading its wings out in masking posture to show it's not about to share this meal with anyone. When it's sure the sparrow is dead it flies off with it. Sorry, sparrows.

On the other hand, sparrow-hawks need to make a living too. They're stunning birds that occupy the top spot in the local food chain and indicate a healthy eco-system. The growing sparrow numbers seem to be able to stand it.

Feb 7th

Mahonia blossom still being visited by queen bumblebees. It's good to know there's a variety of different bee species nearby, including the Tree Bumblebee with its black abdomen and white tail, and the Red-tailed Bumblebee, as well as the Buff-tailed spotted in January. People think bees can only sting once and then die; but female bumblebees can sting repeatedly, though they rarely do. They seem to ignore human beings and animals no matter how close you get to them, just single-mindedly going about their business with that big body, small wings and resultant ungainly flight pattern: bumbling.

Feb 8th

There's a particular cat who knows I will lovingly terrorise it if I see it in the garden, to discourage it from coming in to hunt my beloved wild creatures. But this wily feline has developed a strategy of sneaking in, doing a quick poo on the path and hightailing it out of there. Campaigning against this animal, I now know what it must be like for an army that faces guerrilla warfare with local natives who do hit-and-run raids and melt back into the jungle; it makes them very hard to defeat. And if we don't see the cat's poo we step right in it and then walk it into the house.

I have to admire the animal's tenacity, though – it's almost as intransigent as I am. It's saying: you think this is your territory, but it isn't. You haven't shat here, but I shit here whenever I want. So it's my territory. In fact you've walked my shit right into your house, so your house is my territory too. Guerrilla pooing.

Feb 9th

The seed feeders are especially popular with the small birds at this time of year. The feeder I use has only two perches, so sparrows are continuously contesting who gets to eat at any point in time. There are only one or two individuals in the flock capable of holding a position and fighting off contenders who attack from behind. All the other individuals eat what they can and take off as soon as anyone has a go at them; so there's generally a rapid turnover. Why do I not have a feeder with more perches? Pass.

To me this is an interesting example of the opposing dynamics at work within bird flocks, a paradoxical combination of co-operation and competition or conflict. They look out for one another and give warning when predators are near, and they share information about food sources. But they will fight fiercely with one another for access to food, for the best position within the collective roosting site, for mating partners or nesting sites. Sparrows seem to be squabbling about something or other 95% of the time, but overall gain huge net benefits from being part of the flock.

Maybe we can learn from this. We're herd animals, after all, with same repertoire of co-operation and conflict. Maybe we're doing too much of the conflict and not enough of the co-operation - too much guarding our own personal interests, escalated by vested interests. When this is out of balance, everyone suffers - including the planet. We have a deep instinct to help one another out but it seems to be deeply buried at times like these.

Positioning a bird feeder is important, and the big question in the minds of prey bird species like sparrows is this: is it safe for me to feed here? That's why some people find their newly positioned feeders don't get used. So it's good to place a feeder somewhere quiet with vegetation nearby for cover, but not easily accessed by cats. The perfect situation is where there are branches the birds can sit on as they check it's safe and await their turn to get to feed.

The choice of seed or other food makes a crucial difference too: Nyjer seeds are good for finches; peanuts attract tits and woodpeckers and are also irresistible to squirrels; mealworms are loved by bluetits and robins; black sunflower seeds in their hulls are good for many types of bird, year round; sunflower hearts are popular with everyone and disappear very quickly. Seed mixes can also include all these plus millet or wheat and other small seeds; this is what I use, to appeal to a variety of birds. Of course the gold standard is always to have as much of the food as possible naturally provided within the eco-system itself - like insects and natural seeds - so that the provided food is supplementary as this reduces dependency on human input.

But how is it that some species of birds or animals - known as *monophagists* - can live on a very limited range of food types – sometimes only one specific item – and get everything they need from that, while other creatures including humans have to eat from a very wide range of sources to get the nutrients they need (polyphagists)? Cows and many herbivores can live entirely on grass. Some birds only eat insects; others only eat seeds, and still others only fruit. Some only eat one type of seed or fruit. Goldfinches, for instance, have evolved to only eat seeds directly from seed-heads, such as teasel, thistle, dandelion or sunflower. That is their exclusive ecological niche, as other birds are not equipped with the right pointy bill, so these birds have cornered a market, and it's a food source that continues to be available throughout the winter.

But how can these great differences be? It must be all about transformational capabilities. As all creatures need a wide variety of nutrients, the super-specialists must be able to process their narrow intake in order to provide all these. They will have evolved organ functions that enable them to manufacture those missing vital nutrients internally, or they will host specialised gut bacteria which do that for them – pretty amazing. It's always part of finding a food niche and getting enough from within it. Maximum diversity among these differing options, as ever, enables nature to function best. It's an example of wildlife always comprising a mixture of specialists and generalists of different degree.

We should bear in mind that humans have this amazing transformative gut potential too. It's now known that the thousands of different native bacteria in our biome absorb nutrients according to our food intake, break down toxins, build immunity, affect emotions, and adapt if we change from meat eater to vegan. The microbes here can evolve extremely quickly and adapt to changing circumstances when they're healthy and you have all the right bacteria present. If we keep our gut biome healthy we can get a much greater range of nutrients from our food.

Feb 10th

Another male blackbird appeared recently. Until now the two males seemed to be happily co-existing but today they're disputing the territory, probably because they sense we're already moving out of winter and towards spring when it will be time to get a partner and make babies.

I notice myself feeling somewhat outraged and supportive of 'our' bird. However, studies of blackbird movement have shown that those in our gardens which we think of as 'our' blackbirds – the ones that seem to stay all year– are most often different individuals who frequently migrate round different neighbourhoods and regions; we just can't tell the difference. They probably can't tell the difference between us either. Whatever; I reserve my right to be outraged.

Feb 11th

We now seem to have a pair of grey squirrels setting up home in the garden where there was only one before. It's a dilemma for me as I confess to being something of a grey squirrel disliker and I'm wondering whether to 'discourage' them. Greys often damage trees, stripping bark away to lick the sap, and will eat eggs and often young of small birds. They're bad news for red squirrels, but these have long gone from this area. They've invaded our roof-space and chewed stuff up in the past.

Their colouring seems to vary a lot, ranging from dark grey all over to a dusky reddish colour, sometimes with a white underside and sometimes without. Then there are also all-white examples (known as *leucistic*) and all-black too (*melanistic*). And they all breed like rabbits and seem to like rough sex. Fifty shades of grey squirrel?

Feb 12th

One of the fighting male blackbirds finally won the day and saw the other off. Obviously I'm convinced it's 'our' blackbird who has kept his territory. And now today a hen bird has appeared: the first I've seen one since last autumn. Good news. Maybe her presence is what started them fighting.

Feb 14th

Today I hear a blackbird's soft clucking call: the sound they use when warning a fledgling to stay hidden because there's danger about. But it's completely the wrong time of year for this: why are we hearing it now? Maybe they know it's St Valentine's day. Maybe the male is so enamoured with the female that he's calling her 'baby', like some humans do.

Feb 15th

The pair of bluetits, last seen in January, are about again, this time chasing one another in a prolonged mad dance-flight, twisting and turning in constantly changing directions. The relationship looks promisingly athletic– none of this soppy 'baby' stuff. More signs of imminent spring.

Feb 16th

The pair of collared doves has been frequenting the garden since at least last year, and now they've become all the more infatuated with one another, doing everything an inch or two apart. I'm a bit infatuated with doves myself; they have a substantial adorability quotient and they're admirably loyal to one another.

But – shock horror – today there's an interloper, and he or she is trying to butt in on the cosy relationship. I can't tell the gender. One of the pair doesn't like this one little bit, while the other partner doesn't seem quite so sure. Eventually the three fly off together.

Half an hour later a single collared dove returns. What's going on? Has one of the original pair gone off with the interloper, leaving the partner to return bereft to the territory of which it has such fond memories, hoping that it's only a temporary fling and that the old mate will return, all apologetic?

Feb 17th

A pair of collared doves is back in the garden today with no sign of any third gooseberry bird. But is it the old couple, male dove A and female dove B? Or is it a new couple comprising female dove B and new male dove C? Or even a civil partnership of two male doves A and C? I need to work on my collared dove gender identification skills.

Feb 18th

Magpies [Public Enemy #2, after domestic cats] are suddenly making the garden their base, which they weren't doing before. There are no eggs or fledglings to predate at this time of year, so why now? Are they staking out a claim in advance,

against the local crows? My immediate reaction is to consider discouraging them. Magpies are particularly sensitive to human presence, so all I would have to do is go out into the garden or even just appear at a window and they'll be off. I find that if I repeatedly chase any animal such as cat or magpie, after a few times they get fed up and hang out somewhere less unwelcoming. Its too much trouble. I also hang up a couple of shiny CDs on string; magpies don't like seeing their reflections, especially on moving surfaces.

The RSPB says there's no conclusive evidence to show that magpies adversely affect numbers of other birds long-term, but every spring at fledging time I see them systematically scoffing large numbers of short-lived small birds. And everyone agrees that magpie numbers have increased in these times when just about every other bird population is waning. Apparently one of the major reasons for the steady rise in magpie populations is the relentless increase in car use which results in more roadkill, a favourite takeaway option for magpies that helps them get through the winter.

However, I know I'm not supposed to love some wild creatures and hate others, so I decide to write a list of things I like about magpies. Here it is:

1) they have quite nice colouring and plumage

1) that's it

This isn't working. What I really need is a goshawk that's partial to magpie.

Feb 19th

I filled the seed feeder days ago, but the sparrows haven't touched it: unheard of at this time of year. Is this because of the magpie presence?

Any time I've ever put a new feeder out or moved it to a new position, it will be several days or more before any bird feeds from it. This isn't because it hasn't been noticed – the sparrows see everything as soon as it happens – but because it's not yet been proven safe to eat from. The same thing happens to a lesser degree when a feeder hasn't been filled for a while, such as when we're away on a longer holiday. But this isn't the case here – the seed feeder is in the same position it's been for some years.

Feb 20th

The magpies have ended their residency. I never got around to conducting a serious dissuasion campaign, but they left anyway. What was that all about?

Today I see the hen blackbird gathering nesting material and a pair of sparrows looking into one of the nesting boxes. Breeding season is not far away.

Feb 21st

The birds are at the feeder again, and a single collared dove has been feeding under it each day. Today a blackbird swoops down to feed on the fallen seed, in aggressive mode with tail in the air, seeing off the dove. It doesn't tolerate this bird as competition, yet isn't bothered by twenty or so sparrows doing exactly the same thing. I guess the sparrows are choosing different seed types from the blackbird, but the dove isn't. It's all about having different food niches.

I synchronise putting out the daily winter food with my own breakfast porridge so that I can watch them while I eat as I'm on my own then. It's nice to eat together with the family. The birds wait for this every morning.

Feb 22nd

The routine level of everyday sparrow conflict suddenly escalates today outside my office window among the evergreen clematis that climbs the front of the house. A bunch of half a dozen birds are fighting fiercely a foot or two away from my nose, completely absorbed in internecine warfare, pulling violently at each others' tail feathers and making the loudest sparrow racket I've ever heard; I've never seen this level of vitriol before, even during the mating season. I really don't know what it's about; looks like a bunch of young hooligans getting out of hand. I blame the parents.

I'm always wondering what the sparrows are saying to each other, all the more so since they don't appear to have as much of a range of different calls as most other birds do – just a single 'cheep' sound and repetition thereof. It appears, however, that this call is used with differing intent:

- by males to attract females
- by males to announce they have a nest to offer to a female
- by females to attract a new partner after they've lost one
- in a chattering version, by females chasing off other females
- by either gender as part of courting or during copulation
- by any of them to indicate alarm or anxiety
- by youngsters asking to be fed
- as a single softer note to indicate submissiveness within the flock
- as a general contact call to let someone else know they're there

All these messages are further articulated by distinguishing body language. This is the conventional thinking on the subject, but I reckon there's a good deal of gossip, tale-telling and bad-mouthing, plus males asserting 'I'd be an excellent mating choice for you' and disobedient young with 'I don't have to do what you say, you're not my real father' in there as well.

So it's probably not so much what the sparrows are saying as the way they're saying it; and maybe there are significant differences between the sounds they're making that we're not able to distinguish. They probably observe the same in us as we do in them: that we all sound the same except that some are noisier; that we all look the same, except if you look a bit closer some are males and some are females and some juveniles; and that the females are the alphas and the males are the betas, but the females let the males think it's the other way round.

Feb 23rd

Another woodmouse is living under the old concrete path where I know the slow-worms are hibernating, making regular sorties into the garden for food. Seems to be gathering seeds from under the bird feeder plus a few holly berries that had fallen when birds were feeding on those in the trees. I didn't know this was a woodmouse food item.

This one has such beautiful colouring: golden brown on top, white underneath. I wonder if it's a different individual from our conservatory afternoon-tea-and-cake visitor? You can be near it as long as you stand still: a valuable lesson for nature watching. Go into any natural setting, sit down and stay still, and before very long wild life will resume around you. Most of the people miss most of the creatures most of the time simply because they're passing through and always moving or talking.

Feb 24th

Time to think about nest-boxes again. There's plenty of opportunity for natural nest sites in the dense shrubbery and the creepers that climb the house walls, but I like to add a few supplementary boxes in the hope that I'll get clear views of the birds using them.

The most popular has been the starling box which we installed a couple of years ago under the house eaves; it has a special V-shaped opening which starlings like. It was immediately occupied by starlings but they stopped using it after a couple of years; whereupon sparrows happily took over and have used it ever since. It's rigged up with video so that we can see the occupants live on our telly, all through the stages of taking out old materials and bringing in new, laying eggs and brooding, hatching and then fledging. We invite neighbours' children to watch the key phases as part of our unofficial nature education programme. They love it and it gets them interested in birds.

Nest-box needs vary. Birds like tits and sparrows require a small entry hole around 32mm diameter. Robins, blackbirds, thrushes and wrens prefer open-fronted boxes, well hidden in dense undergrowth. All nestboxes are best placed in sheltered spots away from prevailing wind, rain or direct sunlight, which generally means facing between north and east. Robins, wrens and bluetits like a relatively low level position whereas sparrows and starlings prefer to be high up– hence the popularity of eaves for both those species.

Feb 25th

Sparrows are gathering material and taking it into the hazel tree which is thickly intertwined with honeysuckle and evergreen clematis. So I'm presuming they mean to nest here – I've never noticed them using that site before. I'm seeing them bring twigs they've wrenched from shrubs, dried grass pulled from the ground, old feathers, shredded paper tissues and dry leaves.

Feb 26th

A single belated redwing visitor appears today. There's not much left in the way of berries for it to eat; the earlier flock and the resident blackbirds demolished all those. It quickly moves on. Redwings are distinctly flocking birds; is this one an exhausted straggler that got separated from its flock? Will it manage to find enough fuel to get back to its Scandinavian homeland?

The garden birds are getting spoiled by the quality of the winter food I'm putting out for them, containing dried mealworms and mini suet pellets with insects inside. The male blackbird is always first and always goes for the mealworms. The suet pellets are next most popular, liked by everyone. I'm spoiling them, but it's only for the coldest spells.

Feb 27th

Goldfinches spotted today for the first time this year. They're shy birds, flitting from perch to perch around the garden when no-one else is flying, not staying in any spot for more than a second. They're such beautiful and exotic looking birds with their bold black and white heads, red faces and vivid yellow wing patches. They're always in a small group, usually a family group that includes last year's young.

I was late putting out the mixed bird food this morning. The male blackbird, who watches for me coming out with it at the usual time and is in there like a shot at my feet to get his favourite mealworms, appears at my upper office window and looks in at me working, as if to say, "Where are my ******* worms?" The sparrows too sometimes appear at this window when expected food has not yet been put out.

Feb 28th

Very cold today. Decided to put the suet blocks out instead of the seed feeder for the resident birds, a popular option: instant brown fat for getting through the day, plus reserves for the night. The trouble is, once starlings from the wider neighbourhood find out about it they swoop in like locusts and polish off the lot in seconds. This prompts me to take measures to protect the interests of my in-house residents.

So I've developed a system to deal with this. I put new suet blocks out and then watch. Sparrows will usually start to feed immediately, but as soon as starlings swoop in and chase them away I go out and bring the feeder indoors. I wait fifteen minutes, by which time the starlings will have moved on and won't come back that day. But the sparrows and others are still here; they know the suet feeder will be back out in fifteen minutes, and they'll be straight onto it.

I love systems. I have that system I mentioned in January for growing the garden's super-hedge and for productively disposing of prunings therefrom. I have a system for stopping squirrels emptying the birds' seed feeder. I have another system for helping bumblebees that fly into the conservatory and can't find their way out before they get caught in the spider's webs or fried in the heat: I catch them with a fishing net and release them outside. When ants come into the house I sweep them up with a dustpan and brush and empty them outside so they don't get into the habit of finding food inside the house and making it an established part of their territory. I have systematic ways of dissuading the presence of my less favourite species such as magpies or cats. I have an infallible system for boiling any egg just right. I love systems and I'm not afraid to use them. I'm living the dream.

A little OCD, moi? Undoubtedly.

March

March 1st

Spring is well under way and warm weather predicted for much of the month. The sparrows are in their mating colours. The plumage of house sparrows is mostly shades of grey and brown, giving them good camouflage which they need as a prime prey species; but there are distinctions between the male, female and juvenile and these are more noticeable at this time of year, especially with the male.

The adult male always has bolder colouring than the female, with a black bib and darker brown back with white markings. The adult female has no black colouring, with a lighter brown back and grey body. She is smaller than the male. The juvenile is similar to the female but paler and with a fluffier, scruffier look; it may remain paler till the end of its first year when it is adult and able to breed.

Sparrows are of course extremely gregarious. The individual does a lot of 'social singing' with the flock, calling together for long periods from cover. Sparrows love to tear apart any flowers that are yellow in colour; no-one but them knows why. They fly at 15 wingbeats per second, and can happily swim.

The house sparrow has been living with humans for eleven thousand years. Its split from its closest relative came via a mutation which allowed production of an enzyme called amalay which in turn enabled the bird to digest starch for the first time. This was exactly the same time that humans in the middle-east began settling down and growing agricultural grains which are extremely starchy but which they could now digest. The birds then spread alongside humans with the development of agriculture and the resultant first cities. This niche helped make the bird an extremely successful and widespread species, the most widely distributed wild bird in the world, and widely adopted in human culture as a symbol of lust and sexual potency.

The bird likes to use cavities for shelter and will very often nest under house eaves, but can also manage in diverse other settings such as coal mines 600 metres below ground, and feed on the Empire State Building's observation platform. It does best, though, in wildlife friendly gardens like ours where insects are more plentiful than in city centres or in mono-cultural fields.

Sparrows are highly adaptable; they can learn how to open automatic doors to supermarkets or garden centres to gain entry and reach food sources. Although still relatively common, the house sparrow is in decline and on the Red list for UK species. The decline is now thought to be primarily caused by a strain of avian malaria which is most seriously affecting the southern UK species where mosquito populations are increasing due to temperature rise.

Sparrows don't hold territories, only nests, and then only just before and during the nesting season. Holding onto the nest site in this period is key to sustaining a mating relationship. Nests are usually made from an outer structure of twigs, plant stems and roots, with a middle layer of dried grass and prized bits of string, and an inner lining of softer material such as feathers, animal fur, paper or man-made fabric scraps. Nest making can start well before the breeding season starts, as we've seen in this garden since January. Young sparrows are fed on insects for their first two weeks, after which they can start digesting seeds.

Adult females are known to be dominant over males despite their smaller size: it's a society of alpha females and beta males, a bit like my own household. How do they manage that? Maybe the males are post-feminist. Females fight over the males in the mating season rather than the other way round. Sparrows are generally monogamous but can engage in extra-marital copulation; copulation is always initiated by the female.

March 2nd

Rosa reached 15 years of age yesterday, the equivalent to 105 in human years. Her sense of smell is still excellent. She started barking at something in the garden today as if she didn't know what it was but knew she didn't like what it was doing. I went over and saw it was a big green frog. Maybe she hadn't come across one that size before, or maybe she couldn't understand why it didn't hop away from her as frogs should.

I took Rosa into the house, closed the door and went outside again. I picked up the frog, which didn't seem to mind, and carried it by a circuitous route to the old log-pile in the corner, whereupon it crawled in among the logs. When I went back into the house, Rosa wanted to go back to the frog. I let her out; she went straight back to where the frog had originally been and started sniffing around for it. Not finding any scent trail on the ground, she sniffed the air, picked up the scent there, and with nose lifted high proceeded to follow exactly the route I'd taken with the frog, ending up at the precise point where I had placed it. Working out that the frog was now unfindable, Rosa was happy to call off the search and move on to the next item of interest. And that's why they use cocker spaniels to sniff out drugs.

March 3rd

Nest building is suddenly escalating to fever pitch. In previous years we gathered bits of sheep wool off barbed wire fencing on country walks and hung it up in one of those square suet-block cages, for the birds to pull out and use in their nests. But last year when cutting a hedge back in winter we found that strands of Rosa's moulted hair formed a significant component in the inner cup of some nests, so this year we've been filling another suet cage just with her copious haircut trimmings. When offered the choice of these two nesting materials, the birds have now switched to dog fur and left the sheep wool untouched, perhaps because Rosa's coat is extremely warm and soft whereas the wool has natural grease in it. They empty the cage as soon as it's refilled with the cosy black fur.

The birds' choice here demonstrates a recurring principle in wildlife behaviour: they will use whatever they can get and be perfectly happy with that, but when something better becomes available they'll go for that instead. They're adaptable. It's also another small way in which Rosa and ourselves interactive with the garden's ecosystem.

Different birds have different favourite nesting materials, to provide suitable structure and lining. Sparrows use dry grass as the basic matter, but will always incorporate any feathers, string or paper they can find. Wood pigeons use only twigs, and not many of them at that, in their scanty makeshift little platforms. Blackbirds and thrushes will add a mud lining to their tightly interwoven structure of grass, which will harden into a perfect semi-spherical cup. Robins and wrens like to use moss when available. Some of the tit family tie everything together with spider webs. Sparrows and bluetits use animal or human hair if available. Starlings like wool as a lining.

Why these differing preferences, when they all have access to the same range of raw materials? There's the choice of nest site and the size of the parent and of the eggs and growing chicks which affects choice of structural material, but beyond that the choice of lining material must reflect genetic awareness of the physical needs of each particular specie's hatchlings.

March 5th

Decided to install a small instant wild pond in the garden. Bought a prefabricated unit from a garden centre, with different levels to give different depths, and some native water plants. Dug the right size and shape of hole and used the soil to make a bank behind it. Put the prefab pond in position. End of day one's work.

March 6th

Day two of instant wild pond creation. Lined the mound behind the pond with rocks. Planted native plants around the pond, put the pond plants in and filled with water from the rainwater butt.

March 7th

Day three: users move in! First thing this morning the male blackbird comes to check it out and finds small titbits to eat along the grassy edges, invertebrates disturbed by the digging. He takes a drink and a long splash in the water and when he's finished the hen blackbird gets her turn. By midday the sparrows have discovered it and are drinking and having a bath too.

March 9th

A rare sighting of the male blackbird attacking one of the squirrels: that means he must have something to protect. Eggs? Or future planning thereof?

March 12th

The dawn chorus is in full swing now; it brings so much joy when one is immersed in it. As usual the robin is the first to sing; its large eyes can detect light even before dawn starts; I often see them singing in the town centre when the street lights come on. It's generally the male robin you hear singing, although females also hold territories through winter. The male blackbird is usually the next to sing in our garden. Any wren present comes in when there is full light, followed by bluetits. The chorus ends half an hour or so after full daylight. Sparrows are last; they like a lie-in.

Why do birds sing loudest and most often in the mornings? I understand that it's because the air is coldest and generally stillest then, and sound therefore carries twenty times further than at mid-day. It's probably also about re-establishment of territories after the night.

Friends from New Zealand have come to stay as part of their itinerary of the British Isles. We had been on safari with them in Africa; we wanted to show them the wildlife over here, so we promptly invented the concept of the 'fox safari' and took them on one yesterday evening. We drove around town with torches shining out the windows looking for pairs of green eyes, going to places where we know foxes hang out. We had good sightings of half a dozen different foxes of different ages and conditions; we were able to follow one of them the whole length of our street as it systematically peeled off to check every garden along the way. Our friends loved it.

I'm so glad that decent sized wild animals such as these are able to find a place in our modern towns, and I'm always glad to see one as I cycle or walk around at night. They're admirable adaptors and survivors. They add enormously to the richness of urban wildlife. And they keep rat numbers down in our neighbourhood.

March 13th

Sparrows are nesting all over the shop: under the house eaves, in the dense hawthorn that has honeysuckle growing through it, on the hazel tree with evergreen clematis all over, and in the thick ivy that's in the elder tree; plus the nestbox formerly known as the starlings', and on top of the defunct alarm system box on the house wall, among the regular clematis. All in all, combinations of climbing plants with shrubs and trees seem key to their preferences. They don't need seed feeders at present because of the current abundance of insects

March 15th

7 am. Two robins start fighting hammer and tongs in the air just outside the window I'm looking through, oblivious of everything else. It's vicious; they attack one another with beaks and claws and they're making a din. One suddenly crashes into the window, falls to the ground and lies still. The victor flies off. I go out and pick it up; it's alive, but doesn't struggle.

I bring the stunned bird into the house to see if it will recover. It sits still in my hands for a long time; I can feel its little heart beating and see it gasping for breath. I continue to hold it, but it eventually keels over and a drop of blood oozes from its beak; it must have suffered internal injuries from the fight or from striking the window.

Robins are highly territorial, setting up boundaries to their territories which are invisible to us but well recognised between the birds. A male will then sing to lay claim to his domain, all day long at certain times of year. It will fight off all other birds, often including other species, but the greatest vehemence is saved for any other male robin who dares to cross that line. The fight is often to the death, as my little late friend discovered. Yet they're not at all daunted by human proximity.

Small dead creatures that decay quickly (like this one) go in our compost bin; as in nature, nothing is wasted here. I conduct a brief burial ceremony, honouring its life. That thing about nature being red in tooth and claw certainly applies to robins.

March 16th

It's been interesting to see how over the years one or another plant species can come in and dominate the garden's central patch of open ground for a time and later give way to another dominant species. The current dominator is Herb Robert, a woodland member of the geranium family which likes the mixture of sun and shade that prevails here. It flowers throughout spring and summer, supplying useful nectar for flying insects. Herb Robert has some interesting folk names including Storkbill, Squinter-pip, Stinking Bob and Death Come Quickly. The last term is misleading as it isn't poisonous; indeed herbalists regard is as a valuable enhancer of the immune system; the name probably refers to the way its leaves suddenly turn vivid red when there's a drought.

Brambles are also springing up in the garden; I dig them up and move them into the hedge system to give protection to nesting birds there. Ivy has been climbing up the trunks of the apple, cherry and wild plum trees; is this a good thing? What if it reaches out along the fruiting branches? I decide to let it go for the time being, as ivy is one the very best plants for wildlife. At the crown of each of these trees there is now a dense cluster of the plant, where sometimes birds are showing interest in forming a nest. The squirrel is frequently visiting the most dense clump in the apple tree; I reckon it's using this as a food store as I've seen a magpie checking it out when the squirrel's not there. They don't miss much, those magpies.

In terms of foods for ourselves, favourite foragable plants at present include dandelion, chickweed and Fat Hen.

Another of my favourite plants in full blossom in the garden now is Lesser Celandine, the classic harbinger of spring. It's a member of the buttercup family, with vivid yellow glossy petals and heart shaped leaves. It likes bare ground so is often a pioneer species, expanding its reach each year, mostly through underground tubers separating into new plants. In this way it can make a continuous carpet in woodlands that holds a place in the spring succession ahead of wood anemone and then bluebell. Celandine has a beguiling habit of closing its petals the moment there's cold or rain, then opening again immediately the sky is bright. It's always uplifting to see the blossoms, and makes me feel optimistic.

Wordsworth loved Lesser Celandine so much that he wrote an ode to it:

"Comfort have thou of they merit
Kindly unassuming spirit
Telling tales about the sun
When we've little warmth, or none"

Lesser Celandine is also known as Pilewort – you can guess what that's helpful for. Perhaps Wordsworth had special reason to be grateful to the plant for a very particular type of comfort it brought him.

March 17th

Interaction with our neighbourhood ecosystem has just extended to an exchange of resources with our neighbours across the road. They keep three Indian Running Ducks, delightful creatures that like be cuddled and to come into their house. They also like to eat snails, so I go out on warm and damp evenings to gather some from our healthy population and take them across the road. The ducks go mad for these, swallowing them whole; you can see a series of lumps on their necks where the snails are on their way down. It's a tiny step in the direction of sustainability and self-sufficiency for all of us; the ducks get protein and calcium to form their eggshells and we get a few organic duck eggs in return. The snails are less happy about the arrangement, but I tell them it's nature's way.

There are many examples of this hinterland effect: the value and the influence of species in an urban wildlife garden extending beyond its edges. There are birds and flying insects that spend some of their time in the garden and some in nearby gardens. There are animals like foxes and hedgehogs that roam far and wide, but get something important in this particular spot. There are shrubs, trees and other plants that cast seeds beyond the garden, or whose seeds are carried beyond in diverse creatures' digestive systems.

The garden also produces super abundant stock of creatures and plants that overspill into adjacent areas, and shrubs that we transplant to nearby areas where they are needed. More than this, the idea of having a successful and appealing urban wildlife garden is spread through the neighbourhood by those who pass by, want to know more and then do a bit of wilding in their own gardens.

So this garden contributes in all these different ways to nearby gardens, to the neighbourhood, to the town and indeed more widely than that too.

March 18th

A wren is hopping from twig to twig in the dense lower foliage, just above ground level. I'm now watching out for a possible partner. Few people realise that the wren is the most plentiful of British birds because of its small size, drab colouring, and skulking behaviour; hence the Latin name *Troglodytidis* or cave-dweller. Yet despite the retiring nature its song is loud and can be very complex.

Seeing the bird here in the garden is particularly pleasing as we've made special efforts to make the garden more wren friendly, filling gaps in the lower boundary with hedge-pruning materials and planting creepers there.

I notice this bird continuing to be busy with whatever it's doing right into dusk, later than most diurnal species: maybe just checking out the territory very thoroughly, maybe starting on nest building. The male wren builds many dome shaped nests –up to six – then shows them to a female he hopes to partner with; she will then choose the one they will use. Or find another male.

March 19th

Purchased a smart new nestbox with video built-in and an opening made exactly the right size just for sparrows (like there aren't enough of them for me already, right?) Immediately put it up on a tree in the area where other sparrows are nesting and where they know plenty of food is available. Set it up to show live action on our TV. Likely to be some time before it's occupied as it's brand new and so many other nest sites are available.

March 21st

SparrowCam nestbox has been claimed already! We can see that nest material is being brought in by one or both of a sparrow pair. Such speedy uptake is highly unusual - this one must be considered a hot property. It's immediately obvious that the female is having difficulty fitting through the opening. She's able to do it, but it's a squeeze. Has it been made the wrong size?

March 22nd

Spring equinox dawn chorus: birds start singing at 4am, well before dawn. On this occasion the blackbird starts before the robin, then as we're near the sea come the black backed gulls who are starting to think about nesting on our chimney pots, and finally the sparrows chime in around 6am, which is early for them. Our neighbours discourage the gulls at this time of year by opening their roof window and firing peas past their heads with a catapult; this seems to work, probably because the birds' genetic response makes them think the 'cliff site' nesting spot they're considering must be subject to falling rocks so they should abandon it.

You often hear people call the equinox the first day of spring, but it's actually more like the middle of the season because it marks the mid-point between the winter solstice – mid-winter – and the summer solstice, or midsummer. Of course the actual occurrence of spring phenomena will vary according to how far north or south you are; spring on the south coast of England could be several months ahead of that in northern Scotland. Spring now progresses from the south to the north of the British Isles on average at about two miles per hour or 45 miles per day, taking a minimum three weeks to get all the way there. And the seasons aren't separate anyway; they gradually merge from one to another with short reversions to former weather, so the timing of transition is never a precise or definite matter.

Legendary nature writer Richard Mabey points out that the March equinox marks a much more dramatic seasonal change than the other equinox and the two solstices – as it's the one time of year when all creatures are ready to lurch into reproductive overdrive and all seeking to kill things to feed their young with.

March 23rd

We are seeing material constantly being brought in to the SparrowCam nestbox, yet the net amount isn't building up at all and the central floor of the nestbox is still bare. What's going on?

The male blackbird has suddenly grown still blacker: mating colouring. The female is gathering dead grass for nesting. One of the great things about a totally wild and natural garden - where stuff is never really tidied up - is that there's always plenty of such material lying about, which will have also have helped a healthy stock of invertebrates get through the winter.

March 24th

SparrowCam nest materials mystery solved: someone is bringing material in but somebody else is stealing it. Both bird look like females. Where is the rightful resident's male partner in all of this? Why isn't he doing something about it? Wait a minute, though - we have already established that females are the alpha males in this society.

Our allies the crows (because they're sworn enemies of our worse enemies the magpies) are building a nest in a tree just down the street. And that means they will terrorise any magpie that comes anywhere near their nest site. Good news then for our fledgelings-to-be.

These are carrion crows, *Corvus Corone,* distinguished from the rook by having an all-black beak and living individually or in pairs rather than as a flock. They have a very loud and raucous 'caw' call. These are large, successful and extremely clever birds, and very wary of humans. In urban settings they don't just eat carrion, but also insects, worms, seeds and other birds' eggs.

March 25th

Tiny female hazel flowers are opening, vase shaped buds with red filaments sticking out, no bigger than a pin-head, at the end of the branch tips. Each will then turn, if successfully pollinated from the male catkin flower, into a green sheathed hazelnut by early autumn. Hazel trees are monoecious, which means that they have male and female flowers on the same plant. But they can't self-fertilise. Pollen has to be brought from a separate plant.

A bumblebee is getting nectar from the flowering cherry tree whose petals are just beginning to fall in the bright sunshine. We're now seeing bees other than the queens who are now comfortably ensconced in their nests served by these workers. In years past in this garden pollination was mostly done by common honey bees, but now it's mainly carried out by different species of bumblebee, some social and some solitary. Is this because the latter are doing well here, or because the former are doing less well nationally?

March 26th

The male partner of the resident female sparrow is at last taking an interest in the SparrowCam project and theft of nest material has finally stopped. As a result the net amount is now showing some growth but the central floor area is still bare. More dry grass is appearing now, and the female is appearing with new stuff, departing and then returning quickly. Does that mean egg laying may be imminent?

March 27th

The male too is now feverishly bringing material in to SparrowCam nestbox. The pair chat to one another briefly each time they meet in the nestbox - not their regular cheep-cheep at all, but an impassioned high-pitched squeaky sound. The typical conversation seems to mean something like this: Her: "Bring more stuff in! Quick! Quick!"/ Him: "I am! Stop nagging!

March 28th

Female is now staying put and sitting on the still-rather-bare nestbox floor. She's looking distinctly twitchy. She keeps putting her head under her feathers and sleeping a bit, then waking up and squirming around, then dozing off again. But the male is still bringing more nesting material in. He pokes it into place below her and goes off from more. She seems oblivious to this, just carrying on alternating between twitchy dozing and squirming.

March 29th

5.45am and it's still pitch dark; the blackbird starts to sing its achingly beautiful song. Though I'd rather be still asleep it's a joy to immerse myself in this magical sound. It removes all other troubles from my mind.

Later in the day the male songthrush is singing too - but this time he has found a mate, and as he sings to assert his rights to the territory the female will be making the nest well hidden in deep cover, with its perfectly formed inner clay bowl, soon likely to contain four exquisite sky-blue eggs,

Switching on SparrowCam, I see that there's an egg under the female!

March 30

Now two sparrow eggs. Female is sitting on them, but not continuously. Later in the day I notice two sparrows trying to sit on the eggs at once, side by side, squabbling from time to time and pecking at each other. What's going on? Are these first time parents and the male is wanting to brood too? Or are we also seeing the female who was nicking the nest material and is now pushing for maternity rights? Later still, one of the two has chased the other away, leaving the Real Mum who seems to settle down happily.

I'm also noticing that Real Mum is having less difficulty getting into the nestbox. The laying of eggs must be what's making the difference, which means she must have had some urgency about finding a nest site.

March 31st

Now SparrowCam nestbox has three eggs! So far mum is keeping to the textbook pattern of laying one egg a day, up to five eggs total. But then she clears off. The bottom of the nest under the eggs is still rather bare. Evening draws in and it's going to be a cold night. I can't see her there when I retire at 10.30pm. Will the eggs get chilled and so fail? Has the nest been abandoned? What's going on?

I lie awake reflecting on this and a hundred other sundry existential garden-related emotions welling up from my unconscious: squirrels eating birds' eggs, magpies gobbling fledglings, starlings hoovering up the food intended for smaller birds, robins killing one another, cats staking a claim to the garden with their poo which we then walk indoors, and all the other myriad ways that this precious little haven doesn't fit with my image of how it should really be.

Paranoid, moi? Oui. But with good cause.

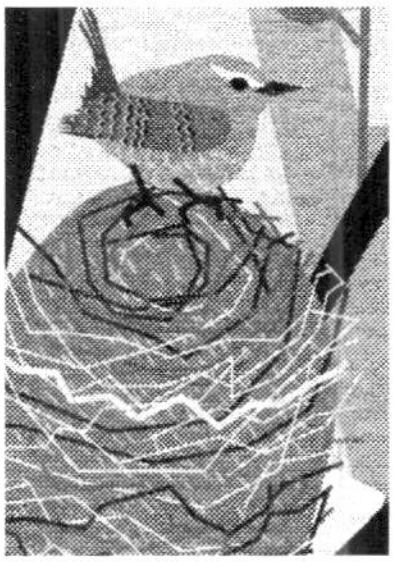

April

April 1st

I confess to being a sparrowphile, probably a sparraholic; I love the little critters; they always make my day. Every month there's something new to learn about them.

Those that are nesting in the eaves of the house are making lots of noise in there; from indoors it sounds like we have hyperactive squirrels nesting in the roofspace, which we've had before – but this time it's just the sparrows. They're nesting all over the garden too - in the older nestboxes, in the house eaves, in the trees and shrubs, on top of the alarm box on the front of the house and in the heart of the neighbour's palm tree. They love the community aspect of nesting close together, which is probably why the new nestbox was so immediately taken up - as well as this particular female rapidly needing somewhere to lay eggs. she knew were on the way. Sparrows are particularly motivated to find new nest sites in this garden as there's so much demand from the expanding flock; and being in the heart of the community with plenty of natural food onsite is crucial.

And today there are four eggs in the SparrowCam nestbox. The parents are each taking turns to sit on them while the other brings in more nest material, especially feathers. at this stage. Is this the beginning of the hatching phase? It's interesting to see the male now playing a more constant role, perhaps sparked by completion of the egg laying phase. The female is doing a bit more of the sitting and the male a little more of the bringing-in-stuff DIY.

It's interesting to see the different breeding strategies of the various bird species unfold in the spring. The sparrows, for instance, have multiple chicks in their broods and so can cope more easily with losing one or two; in the flock they have many eyes looking in many directions to protect many fledglings: they and other small birds like bluetits use the 'large numbers' breeding model. But the blackbirds nesting in this garden tend to end up with just two or sometimes only one fledgling; they have no other blackbirds looking out for them. As a result they're highly protective of each individual, keeping them hidden in cover until they're young adults, and giving an articulate variety of warning calls when danger of differing levels is present.

April 3rd

Oh dear. Today, while Rosa was having a roam round the garden and I wasn't paying attention, she discovered and rapidly destroyed a family of baby woodmice. Mea culpa. I don't know whether she made a snack of them, but the nest in the undergrowth was trashed. I shall keep an eye on her bowel movements and any regurgitations over the next twelve hours. Hopefully the mice will breed again.

April 4th

All through winter and then spring, whenever I have put food out for the birds, I would notice the solitary male robin turning up at regular feeding time. waiting patiently until other species had eaten, and then finding his share. But today for the first time as he sits on his usual waiting perch, I see that he has a partner alongside him. I'm delighted as I know this highly interactive bird very well as he always joins me when doing gardening work.

April 5th

Several queen bumblebees are looking for nesting sites to start their new hives, coasting round at ground level and zooming in to look closely at the ground every now and then. Their optimum site will be a disused mouse hole, which they will probably find by smell. This is why when you buy one of those commercial wooden bumblebee boxes they tell you to get the straw from an old woodmouse nest, as if this was the easiest thing in the world. Both bees and mice must have evolved in tandem so that the old dry bedding material contains the right sort of bacteria - or antibacterials - for the bees to set up home and breed in. These queens have a good chance of doing well in our garden as woodmice are a constant presence. Good choice by them.

I'm learning that sparrows have a much greater range of call sounds than I previously thought, through observing and listening them on the SparrowCam TV link. When the parents are doing their regular brooding changeover, and when the female is sitting, she will often make a short whistling call that I've never noticed before, which seems to mean that she wants something from her partner. He mostly appears immediately, so he must be spending time hanging around waiting to be told what to do, maybe a bit like dad at the scene of human birth, not quite sure where to put himself. I'm guessing this whistling call variously means "Come and take your turn sitting on the eggs", or "Bring me some food" or - as it sounds more annoyed, "You're ****ing useless!"

If the male doesn't immediately appear when thus summoned then she will switch to a strident, repetitive version of normal sparrow cheeping for a while. But if he still doesn't show up she will leave the nest for a bit, presumably to get food. There's also a special call to the brooding bird which either parent can use from outside the box, which seems to be saying "I'm here with food" or "I'm ready to take over". Both parents will never be in the nest with eggs at the same time. When a successful handover takes place between the parents they will engage in a rapid cheeping dialogue. Finally I've noticed a throaty rachetty call which seems to be an aggressive warning against any unwanted intruder.

The incoming bird will always bring in additional nesting material, which is interesting considering that the eggs were laid some days ago now, and you'd expect the nest building to have been completed ahead of the hatching stage. But then there was that Great Nest Robbery at the beginning of the cycle. What I don't know is how experienced these particular parents are: is this their first go at reproduction and are they making it up as they go along? I'm hoping that the female's early intermittent sitting on the eggs was the right thing to do - providing enough heat to stop the eggs chilling at night but not enough to set any of them into hatching mode until all were laid.

I've also noticed the eggs are steadily becoming shinier as both parents continuously squirm down onto them to generate heat. Laying is definitely finished; the question now is, when are they going to hatch? The textbook says 11 to 14 days from end of laying to hatching. but like most wild creatures these sparrows probably haven't read the book.

April 6th

Last night we took Rosa out for a quick walk round the block before bed: on coming back through the garden she started barking at something; it was a large hedgehog. Rosa's never seen one of these. She just kept barking, as with the frog last month, and the hedgehog just stayed there, not curling up but just standing still, so obviously not too freaked out. We brought Rosa inside and went outside to watch the hog, in a state of excitement; a hedgehog visiting your wild garden is something you keep hoping for - and trying to provide the right conditions for - but whether it happens or not is beyond your control. This is our first.

As we stood watching quietly it began to move. It sniffed around the spot it was at, found something and chomped on it, then sniffed around to find more of whatever delicacy that was. It wasn't bothered by us; hedgehogs don't have great eyesight. Then I noticed something small and white fall down in front of the hog; it sniffed round, found the white thing and ate it. Then it dawned in me that this scenario was happening right below the live mealworm feeder I'd been putting out for birds to provide soft invertebrate food to feed their chicks.

As we watched, every now and then a worm would manage to climb up the side of the feeder and over the edge, then fall to the ground. It seemed the hedgehog knew about this and was taking advantage. This would mean that on any day when the robin or other birds hadn't eaten eat all the mealworms, this hedgehog had learned that it could turn up and feast on them. And we had no idea. It must have been going on for weeks. From that day on, poor old Robin didn't get any more mealworms; we put them out after dark, just for the hedgehog, whose presence here at all must mean that we're doing something right.

Hedgehogs eat a wide range of ground invertebrates including worms, slugs, beetles, caterpillars and centipedes, as well as supplementary items such as fallen fruit, bird's eggs, frogs and even baby rodents whenever they can get them. Live mealworms are a firm favourite, but they shouldn't eat too many of them - just a delicious snack. They have poor eyesight but good hearing and strong sense of smell.

The last time I'd seen a hedgehog in this vicinity was late one evening in the middle of last winter. I'd been walking home from the pub along our street, and got nearly home when I noticed a small shape shuffling along, staying close to the line of garden fences. It was a tiny hedgehog; I had thought to myself: there is no way this creature is big enough to get through the winter. So I picked it up – it curled up in the time-honoured manner – put it in my backpack and took it home to decide what to do. Back home I weighed it; it was only 300 grams, well below the minimum weight required to survive winter. I put it in a box overnight with a bowl of water and some live woodlice to snack on.

In the morning I rang the local animal rescue service and asked what I should do. They said they had an arrangement with our local vet; I could leave it off there; they would test its health and remove any parasites. If it was healthy enough they would then deliver it to the rescue centre where it would be fed through the winter. I called later to check what had happened and all had gone according to plan. It's highly unlikely that this animal would have survived for long, having to go out and find scarce food when it should have been asleep for most of the winter and living off bulky body reserves. How great that both the rescue centre and out local vet offer this service free of charge. The general guidance is that if you see a hedgehog out and about in daytime it's probably in trouble.

April 7th

All wildlife activity is stepping up a notch in this fecund season - feeding, multiplying, predating and trying to escape from predation. All the birds, animals and insect populations are more visible and daring than usual as they're fired up by reproductive hormones. Everyone's body language is more demonstrative and flamboyant, very different from the usual economy of movement and trying not to be noticed by predators. It's a totally frenzied cornucopia.

I know the pair of blackbirds is building a nest as I've seen each of them pulling dry grasses and carrying them away, but they go to great lengths to hide the location. Even when they think no-one can possibly be looking they will always enter the shrubbery some distance from the nest site and then travel there inside the foliage. And they'll usually choose a nesting place with particularly dense cover. But over a period you get a rough idea where the nest must be.

Sparrows, by contrast, don't seem to care who sees where they're nest building; the nest sites will become common knowledge before very long anyway with all their chattering and bickering. In these ways the blackbirds and the sparrows are expressing their two very different breeding strategies mentioned above.

April 8th

I'm privy to a couple of surprising incidents today. First, the squirrel climbs up onto the fence; the male blackbird nearby isn't having that and chases it away. Usually the squirrel will be dominant. Then a collared dove sees off a magpie - also a reversal of usual status.

I wondered what's the story behind these unusual behaviours. After keeping watch I saw that the dove I'd seen was hanging around another one which was sitting on a nest. So that was it; the male is chasing away intruders to protect the eggs under the female. And the blackbird must have thought the squirrel was too close to its own top secret nest site. Many birds will take on aggressors they would normally avoid challenging or be fearful of, when their eggs or young their are threatened. This tactic must work most of the time otherwise they wouldn't take the risk. The magpie could probably get the eggs if it stuck to the task, but having the two doves to get past is causing it to look elsewhere to find an easier meal – such as eggs that are un-guarded.

Other commonly seen examples of this risky tactic include smaller birds seeing off predators such as crows, owls and even buzzards. This can expand into mobbing when other small birds join in the attack, and that can include dive-bombing. Many species have a special 'mobbing' call which they only use when under attack, in order to get others to quickly join them and defend the common interest. But nobody goes as far as trying to see off a sparrow-hawk, goshawk or peregrine.

April 9th

Slow-worms are living under the old concrete paving slabs that form the path through the garden. These were laid in 1948 when the house was built, so there now are lots of cavities that provide them with ideal hibernation quarters from October to March, and sleeping places for the rest of the year. We see them when they come out to bask in the sunshine to raise their blood temperature enough to be able to get on with hunting for food. They live on invertebrates such as slugs, snails, worms and spiders, all of which abound in the garden, so we have a healthy slow-worm population.

These small legless lizards are often mistaken for snakes, especially as they have a forked tongue which they stick out to detect scents in the air. I love their burnished metal look which can vary in colour from green to grey to bronze.

April 10th

The male sparrow is still bringing in additional nesting material to the SparrowCam nestbox, mostly grass and feathers. He now places it on top of the eggs, but the female - who is now doing all the brooding - is pushing it under the eggs and then snuggling down again. I'm convinced that the female is now talking to the eggs, making a very soft clucking sound as she settles down onto them. There must be good evolutionary reasons for doing this.

The blackbird pair are finally letting us get occasional glimpses of a fully fledged brown juvenile in their very attentive care. The male is feeding his own favourite food - dry mealworms from the supplementary seed mix we're still putting out - to his youngster. He won't let his wife have any of these, and never has.

April 12th

We've been away for a couple of days. Now we're back it's immediately obvious that something strange is happening in the garden – or rather, not happening. We can't see any sparrows and we're not hearing their usual chatter from the shrubbery. Indeed there don't seem to be any birds around at all. It's eerie. Stranger still, there's still seed left in the feeder from before we went away; I've topped it up today but nobody's eating it. It looks like the whole sparrow flock has moved away en masse – is that possible? What's going on?

But don't worry - the female is still sitting on the SparrowCam eggs.

April 14th

Still no sign of the rest of the sparrow tribe, though the blackbirds are now in evidence again. This is strange and worrying. The SparrowCam female is relentlessly brooding, and presumably getting takeaway food brought in by hubbie.

Sure enough, later today the four eggs are hatching. Sparrow eggs are tiny - just 22 mms long and 15mm diameter, about the size of my smallest fingernail and weighing just 3 grams - so the birds are the same size upon hatching. They're about fifty percent mouth and fifty percent body (we all know people who are a bit like that) completely bald and not a pretty sight. Little aliens. They can hardly lift their heavy little heads but nonetheless immediately start struggle to do this to reach for food. Both parents are immediately busy bringing in insects for them.

April 15th

Phew! Starting to see and hear the rest of the sparrow tribe again; I think I've worked out what's happened. Sparrow-hawks are sensitive to human presence, and I know they keep an eye on the garden and attack from time to time. I reckon our local hawks, needing to feed their young and finding themselves undisturbed in our absence, came in for an opportunistic kill, then must have returned a number of times, which would have freaked the sparrows out and driven them to move into nearby gardens and hide there, not even coming out for food. But now that we're back the hawk is probably hunting elsewhere. Normal service is gradually resuming.

This is why sparrows are so very alert every second they're out in the open; you can see them constantly twisting their heads in rapid jerky movements to look about in every direction, especially upwards. They know they're a popular prey species; perhaps they've twigged how sparrow-hawks got their name. If a flock is gathered on the top of a shrub and a predator is spotted, they will all instantly drop down into the protective heart of the shrubbery, especially favouring thorny species such as hawthorn for this reason.

Even nestlings display this response. When the silhouette of any bird of prey passes overhead they will instinctively duck down into the depths of their nest. How can they know to do this when they've never seen a hawk or even know what it is? The same genetic memory applies in other ways too; crows, magpies and wood pigeons will fly off on the lowest possible trajectory if they see you holding a stick up in the air, resembling a gun; the birds that didn't have this response haven't bred because they've been shot. This applies equally even if the bird has never been shot at in its life, which is the case with urban birds such as ours.

So my question is: do humans too have this capability? The answer is yes; all animals –indeed all living organisms – have *epi-genetic* memory deriving from their ancestral surroundings, which supports them in adjusting to changing environments they may be born into. It's stored in their DNA sequence; this capability is referred to as *phenotypic plasticity*, and plants have it too. This is how we can know things we never learned, and how we have pre-conditioned reflexes which our brain comes with ,factory-installed.

Sea turtles, just hatched, know instinctively to move towards the sea. Honeybees already know how to do the waggle-dance to let other bees know where they got nectar. Male sticklebacks will attack anything red during mating season. Sparrows and thrushes learn their songs by listening to their peers, but other birds such as flycatchers come with a complete and complex singing vocabulary already pre-installed in their system at birth. Millions of monarch butterflies each year make the 2,500 mile journey all the way from Canada to a precise part of Mexico and then back again. But here's the thing: it takes three generations of these amazing insects to make the total journey, so no individual experiences the whole route and none can learn it for re-use. The memory is collective and genetic. Likewise, six-month-old humans and babies are frightened of spiders and snakes by default. The majority of husbands are scared of their mother-in-law; perhaps it's in their DNA.

April 16th

The SparrowCam hatchlings are now producing white poo sacs which the parents religiously dig out from under them and dispose of well away from the nest site. It's a terrific evolutionary feature; if only we humans had developed this faculty we wouldn't have landfill sites full of disposable nappies. The little ones are total eating and pooing machines, ceaselessly reaching up to demand food anytime a parent darkens the doorway from first light until dusk, and sometimes during the night too when the brooding adult stirs a little in sleep.

Three unfeasibly cute tiny fox cubs have been born just up the road from our house and are now coming out with their mum to play in the street every late evening when there's hardly any traffic. They must be barely a month old, which is when they first come out, after being born in mid-march. At birth foxes are blind, deaf and almost bald and so cannot be left alone at all for their first two weeks of life. More than half young foxes die before they reach ten months of age, and few live longer than a couple of years.

These youngsters are extremely agile and can already climb over any fence their mum can get over. They're local celebrities; the street WhatsApp group is full of video clips of their antics. They're such a delight. I suppose finding young creatures generically lovable is another of our human ancestral genetic responses.

April 17th

Without meaning to, it turns out I've rescued a bird from death by sparrow-hawk.

Walking into the garden first thing this morning I disturbed the returned hawk which was close by at the foot of the side hedge. I immediately noticed that a starling was having a go at it: now that's something I've never seen. Caught by surprise, the hawk flew away down along the edge of the hedgerow, closely followed by the starling; I could see it was carrying something. In an instant the hawk had reached the bottom of the garden, done a tight turn along the back hedge, wheeled out through the narrow gap where the gate is, and was gone. But it dropped whatever it was carrying. I walked over to the spot and looked into the long grass; there was a young starling, lying on its back with claws extended in the air and mouth wide open. It was developed enough to have feathers rather than downy fluff, but the wing and tail feathers were short so it wouldn't have been capable of proper flight.

I picked up the bird and held it; it didn't resist in the slightest, just lying on its back in my hand, perfectly still with its mouth wide open and feet still sticking upright. It was breathing and still clearly alive. I held the bird and watched; I reckoned it was suffering from shock and shortage of breath. After a few minutes it seemed to grow calmer and its beak wasn't so wide open. I began to examine it to see what damage had been done. Both wings appeared unbroken, but when I started checking one of its legs it clutched at my finger with that claw, with surprising strength, and did not want to let go.

This was a surprisingly heart-rending moment for me; I knew it was probably just trying to defend itself while regaining its breath, but it wasn't struggling or protesting. It felt to me for all the world like that human situation when a new-born baby so endearingly clutches your finger with its tiny hand, exerting an astonishingly amount of strength and tenacity and peering at you. For me it was one of those powerful and magical moments when you make a deep connexion with another of nature's beings, and it goes right to your core - a moment you will remember vividly for the rest of your life. Quite frankly, I was deeply in love with this little being; maybe it was in love with me - who knows what it was thinking or feeling.

The same thing happened when I finally extricated my finger and test the other leg; but still the creature lay on its back and didn't struggle. When I'd extricated that second finger, the fledgling finally began to move; I placed it on the ground the right way up and it immediately ran into the safety of the hedge bottom. The mother had watched the whole thing from a branch overhead. Her feathers had been visibly damaged by her scrap with the sparrow-hawk, which - against all the odds - had turned out the way she wanted.

Knowing that moments like this can happen at any time is a big part of why we do wildlife gardening, don't you think?

April 18th

The SparrowCam nestlings are growing extraordinarily fast and are starting to be hairy with their first down. For their first ten days of life they cannot regulate their own temperature and so are reliant on the parents sitting on them when it's cold. I don't know how they manage to breathe and avoid getting squashed.

A big V-shaped flock of geese flies overhead, honking loudly. The author and aviator Antoine de Saint-Exupery reported that when wild geese are seen migrating over a farmyard containing chickens, the latter will jump into the air and try to fly south. More memory in the genes?

But as well as any traces of genetic memory these birds - and other migrating creatures such as salmon - also require *magno-reception* to orientate the path they need to take in relation to magnetic north. This sense operates by virtue of small receptors in their organs and blood, containing minute traces of the mineral magnetite which responds to the earth's magnetic field. Even embryonic salmon which have not yet hatched have this in their bodies, ready to come into use when they're much older. It's thought that humans have this capacity too, but it's fallen out of use in recent eras of evolutionary (alleged) progress. Dogs have magno-reception as well; you may have noticed that their preference when doing a poo is to align their bodies along the north-to-south magnetic axis whenever possible. Rosa, it seems, hasn't heard about this; she poos while continuously going round in a circle. So it seems that humans have the capacity for magneto reception but have evolved away from using it.

April 19th

Every creature in the garden seems to be in a frenzy of reproduction and noisiness, a veritable sexfest involving the other sparrows, the robins, the woodpigeons and doves. It's, like, totally fecund. Even as I write this journal, from my upstairs office I observe a pair of sparrows vigorously having it off on the windowsill. The female behaviour when inviting mating - and it's always she who calls the shots - is very much like how the fledgeling expresses desire for food: wing-flicking, incessant cheeping, hopping up close to the chosen male.

Haven't seen the squirrel for a while. I presumed she must be preoccupied with looking after young, but upon enquiring with neighbours I learned that she had been captured by a nearby gardener whose trees were being damaged. She has been taken to a faraway place and released. She's certainly not going to be happy about that, especially if she's leaving young ones behind. And grey squirrels let you know in no uncertain terms when they're not happy; they go mad, have a hissy-fit and can give you a nasty bite. Let's see what happens next.

April 20th

We're in a heat-wave. We're keeping our conservatory doors open to avoid over-heating, and this has prompted the sparrows to develop a new feeding pattern. Spiders are their all-time favourite food item – especially at this time of year when their youngsters only eat invertebrates - and the conservatory houses spiders with webs along its roof timbers. Now the sparrows have learned that they can fly right inside and get easy spider-pickings (or maybe the Sumerian hosts of their ancestors six thousand years ago had conservatories and they're just drawing on that epigenetic memory?) We're more than happy to see this; those spiders' webs catch and kill a considerable number of bees and butterflies that find their way into the conservatory looking for nectar-bearing plants.

Spiders' webs are extraordinary. How do the creatures not get stuck on their own sticky filaments while making them? Apparently they have a system to prevent this: they lay out the major straight structural lines of the web between anchoring points using silk that isn't sticky, then lay a non-sticky spiral system across these. That provides a safe pathway for them to lay another spiral, this time sticky, going in the opposite direction. Clever. The wasp spider has seven different types of silk for different parts of her web.

We're chuffed that the sparrows will come into the conservatory and go about their business even when we're sitting there having a cup of tea. I've no doubt they recognise that we're the humans they see every day and reckon that if we were going to do them harm we'd have done it by now. And we're the people that put out food for them in hard times.

April 21st

First holly blue butterfly of the year, visiting the tiny white holly flowers for nectar: another of my favourite markers of the seasons.

First ever damselfly in our garden – and it flew right into the conservatory, no doubt looking for insects to predate upon. Looked like an Emerald Damsel, *Lestes Sponsa*. Beautiful.

Unlike dragonflies, these brightly coloured insects fold their wings in to the body when stationary. They prey upon smaller flying insects such as mosquitoes, gnats and fruit flies, which they ambush from cover rather than catching while patrolling on the wing as dragonflies do - a very welcome job.

April 22nd

A pair of goldfinches nested recently on the outer tip of a tree branch outside our garden so that predators couldn't get at them; but this carries the risk of the nest being blown away by wind, and that's what just happened. Back to square one for them.

April 23rd

The hedgehog's visits have prompted me to get a Springwatch style trailcam with infrared vision to set up in the garden and see what goes on and who comes to visit by night. Am putting it out tonight for the first time

April 24th

Wild foraged species for our own consumption from the garden this month have included nettle tops, sow thistle, dandelion leaves, chickweed and wild carrot.

The resident hen blackbird, chased by goodness know what – sparrow-hawk probably – crashes into the window as I'm looking out, and collapses on the ground, unconscious. I pick her up and bring her into the house so that she doesn't get nabbed if the predator's still around. One of her tail feathers is damaged. I hold her in my hands; she raises her head and looks at me. She begins to stir a little, but doesn't struggle and doesn't seem to be in a hurry to go anywhere. She must have been stunned; but is she also injured? I hold her a while longer; then she starts to stand up and look around her. I take her outside, put her on a low roof and stay nearby keeping watch. After a few minutes she flies off. I'm pleased and I imagine she is too.

April 26th

The SparrowCam fledglings are growing at very different speeds, with some now showing feather cases among their straggly down. Those that push themselves forward - and so get most of the food - steadily become stronger and are consequently better at climbing over the top of the others - and so it goes on.

I've been amazed to see the trailcam video footage from the last few nights; I had no idea there was so much wild nocturnal traffic passing through. The first thing I saw was that 'our' hedgehog - a male, I believe - doesn't just come once in a night

– he returns periodically, at different times on different nights. In another clip there's a cat in the frame with him, and she seems extremely edgy; I guess it's pitch black and the cat isn't too sure what animal is right beside her. Odd foxes pop in at different times, and in one case there are two foxes at once. But the hedgehog is never seen in the same video clip as any fox; I presume he disappears and comes back later if he smells a fox. Most excitedly, another smaller hedgehog also appears: a potential female partner? Exciting stuff.

April 27th

The SparrowCam fledglings are rapidly developing: wing and tail feathers are emerging out of their cases on the fastest growing individuals. These ones are doing a lot of preening and scratching to facilitate this process. They're also more mobile, developing stronger legs, moving around the nestbox and not staying huddled together in the corner for warmth. The biggest are about half the size of their parents. Mum is finding it ever harder to get under them to find the poo sacs while being relentlessly mobbed for food. But she's thorough and persistent in this task, knowing that it's important for their wellbeing and development.

The garden is full of different kinds of fledgling, each with flicking or quivering wings, incessantly following parents round and calling for food: a risky strategy. Both robin parents are into their ' flyer program : flying into the dense hedge at human eye level, to feed their young with insects at regular thirty second intervals from 6am to 9pm ,when it's getting very dark. So they must have a decent sized brood of fast growing chicks.

Magpies are intercepting the very youngest sparrows directly as they fledge from their nests. One of the magpies is mobbed by a whole gang of sparrows as it flies off with a fledgling in its beak; too late for that one, I imagine, but I guess the sparrows can at least make if difficult for the predator, and there's a small chance they might make it drop its prey.

The crows are doing Bad Things too: one of them attacked the pet rabbit belonging to our duck-owning neighbours across the road. The rabbit was in its hutch but was curious about the crow and came up to the wire mesh, whereupon the crow pecked at its eyes. The crow had been hanging around for a week or two so I encouraged the neighbours to do a campaign of discouragement to persuade this corvid to look elsewhere for somebody's eyes to peck out. The eyes of a magpie would by my choice.

April 28th

A crow claims the first fledgling victim I've seen – a sparrow or other small bird - the downside of having the crows nesting close by. But they don't seem to harvest fledglings on anything like the scale the magpies do. I believe they prefer bigger prey like young doves or pigeons.

In the SparrowCam nestbox, however, all seems to be going to plan. The young are beginning to look like sparrows for the first time. Most of them are now cheeping for food rather than just having constant gaping beaks; in fact they call for food every second or two no matter whether anyone is there to hear them, all day and into the night, perpetually driven by sibling competitiveness. This seems like a waste of energy as they seem to throw their whole bodies into it, but it must work. Maybe it's similar to the way human children get what they want - by wearing the parents down.

There's lots of wing-stretching and as they grow it's getting increasingly crowded. They're having to flap themselves up to the nestbox hole to get food as Mum is not now coming inside except for poo sac collection. Only one nestling can be at the opening at a time; those who stay at the back never get any of the food, so the differential between the individuals is becoming ever greater, with the largest twice the size of the smallest.

Mum also seems to be feeding them less often - is she doing this to encourage fledging soon? This has caused the youngsters to start looking round the bottom of the food for items that might have got missed - early beginnings of foraging instinct and self-feeding behaviour.

Watching all this is daytime TV of the highest order, giving a forensic level of insight into their lives day and night. It's intriguing, dramatic, touching, suspenseful and poignant: a soap opera with the rare quality of being authentic and convincing.

April 29th

Only the very smallest SparrowCam fledgling is now cheeping constantly for food - it doesn't seem to have learned that it's obtained by fighting your way to the front and flapping up to the nestbox opening when an adult is nearby with a delivery. And of course that's why it's the littlest; the system seems to be based on the quasi-biblical principle of 'to him that hath shall be given more'. It seems harsh, but at an evolutionary level must make sense. The bigger nestlings have learned to save their energy in order to be first up there when the light is blocked by an approaching parent. The parents are now in the habit of staying outside the nestbox with a beakful of insects that will feed several youngsters, and then waiting for them to successively appear and giving a little to each.

A neighbour calls me from across the road to say that a young collared dove is in the middle of the road, and can I come and conduct it to safety? It's not yet flying and is being closely watched by both parents, but keeps wandering back every time we shoo it away from the traffic. So I pick it up – it doesn't struggle at all and the parents don't get agitated - and take it to a dense tree nearby and place it on a secure looking branch, where it stays. I can see that the parents are tailing us, and as soon as we leave they fly in to join it. I guess that's all we can do at this stage. The neighbour is going to keep an eye on things. Try doing that with a corvid or seagull nestling – you'll know all about it from the parents. This is all part of our comprehensive nature rewilding service.

April 30th

The robin pair's frenzied feeding trips to the nest has suddenly ceased; the babies must have fledged and the family no longer be centred on the nest site.

"Nature spends her whole genius on the least work," said Henry Davie Thoreau, author of the early nature classic *Walden*. We can see infinite complexity in the tiniest creation and infinite fascination in the most mundane creature. It would appear that the average size of all creatures of all sizes - over the whole planet - is less than that of a housefly. The wonder of it all.

The hedgehog has been coming each evening for mealworms, regular as clockwork. I think he's got into the habit of waiting in cover for the mealworms to appear in the appointed spot at the regular time, directly on the ground and lit up by our porch light. There's now an established procedure which he seems to recognise: 1) I take Rosa out for her last walk and toiletries; 2) I bring Rosa back inside; 3) I bring the mealworms out and put them in the appointed place; 4) I step back out of the light and wait; 5) Mr Hedgehog immediately steps out of the shadows and starts munching.

I only put maybe a dozen worms out as they're rather rich, and too many can upset the hog's digestion. When he's snuffled round and satisfied himself that he's found them all he continues on round the garden finding woodlice, which abound under the dense thatch of foliage on the ground. I've taken to standing and watching this creature every evening, often for quite a long time. He's just going about his everyday business, quite oblivious me or at least not bothered.

The impact of this experience took me by surprise at first. It brings a most extraordinary feeling of profound happiness: a sense that, just for these fleeting moments, everything in my world seems perfect, that all my worldly worries are forgotten, that nothing could be changed to make things any better. Having this iconic animal here seems like the epitome of wild naturalness. Maybe it's because this species is so scarce and therefore all the more special; or perhaps it's the fact that hedgehogs are just about the most heart-achingly adorable creatures you'll ever encounter. Maybe it's all of these.

But it's also a feeling of deep deep love for this creature for whom we are honoured to be able to offer support. This is where things get transcendental; in these moments I love this hedgehog as much as I love anyone or anything in this world. Standing there watching it, everything else is forgotten. I'm in a state of bliss. I could stay out all night; but eventually he always wanders out the gate and off somewhere else.

With that love comes a deep-seated urge to preserve and protect all these creatures that visit the garden, in the face of the forces that we as humans are relentlessly bringing to bear on them. That's what this wildlife garden is about. What a privilege.

Sentimental, moi? Bien sure.

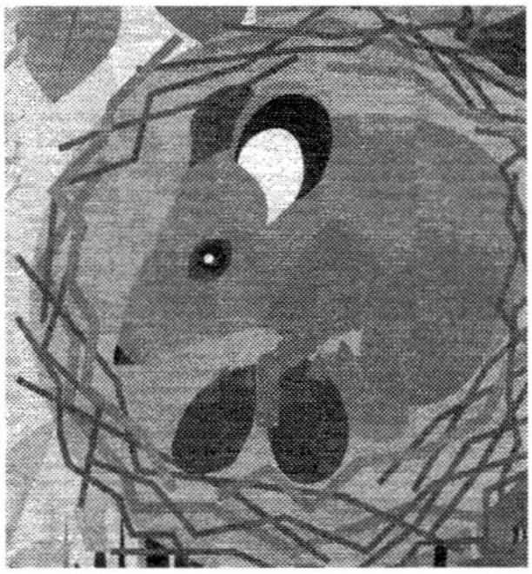

May

May 1st

The heat continues. The hen blackbird whom I looked after last month still has the damaged tail feather but otherwise seems to be fine; I see her out and about gathering food, presumably for one or more young waiting in the foliage to be fed. She clearly recognises me and has become altogether unfrightened and will feed right beside me. I wonder how long this will last?

But despite the heat it's fledge day in the SparrowCam household which started at dawn and has continued through the day till all but the smallest nestling has departed. They're tempted out by the parent sitting on a branch near the nestbox with a beakful of tasty insects, but not delivering it to the bird clinging to the inside of the box with its head sticking out. One of the refinements of this system is that the little ones are not encouraged out until they stop tweeting, thus reducing the attention of predators.

Still seeing Mr Hedgehog in the evenings.

May 2nd

The last SparrowCam nestling, still cheeping away and being fed by one of the parents while the other looks after the three fledgelings, has had its first night alone. It was huddled in the back corner of the box with its head tucked back round under its feathers, as it's parents did at night when they were there. Being on its own at night will hopefully add persuasion to leave soon. This one has always lagged behind the others - from the start it has been less strong, less competitive, and often facing the wrong direction to get food when it came in. Its tail and wing feathers are still rather short. Let's see if my theory about not encouraging wee ones out until they stop cheeping is right.

I hadn't realised how good sparrows are at catching insects in the air. Today it's the mosquitoes emerging in numbers towards dusk around the rainwater butt which contains a good population of their larvae. So at the end of this very warm day when there are many young insect-craving young mouths to feed and the mozzies are doing their mating dance flight, all the sparrows I can see are systematically hunting them in mid-flight. They also do a neat trick of catching additional insects when they already have some in their beaks; how do they do that? Those youngsters who have already fledged are sitting on branches, wing-flicking and incessantly calling to be fed. That's a good idea if you want to attract the attention of predators.

The sparrows are also skilled at pulling the first tiny pears off the tree; are they eating these, or are they looking for insects? Either way I'm not bothered because pear trees are notorious for producing too big a crop and thus exhausting themselves for the following year when there will then be a negligible crop, thus setting up an alternating two-year cycle of feast and famine. The conventional solution is to cull a good proportion of the tiny fruits in the abundant year, which we don't need to do because the sparrows are kindly doing that. Sparrows are always doing something interesting, and doing it energetically. Their lives are short but they pack a lot in. They just seem so enthusiastic all the time, whatever they're doing. I love it.

May 3rd

Checking on the telly video link, I see that SparrowCam nestbox is empty: I'm calling the baby sparrow Elvis because he's left the building.

Later in the day I find Elvis sitting on the garden path, hopping about in the open which isn't a great idea. I'd prefer him to have fled from me into the foliage, which I eventually encouraged him to do.

Had to prune back the outer shrubby hedging today as it now overhangs the street pavement too much. In the course of doing so I was cutting closer to the collared doves' nest that I knew was there and didn't want to disturb them. So I kept an eye on the female who was sitting on eggs throughout, and she didn't seem bothered at all. She sat still and looked calm even when my pruning line was close against the nest. I suppose she either: 1) recognised me and knew I wasn't a threat; or 2) was determined to stay on her eggs come what may; or 3) was pretending she wasn't there and hoping I couldn't see her. Doves and town pigeons seem to be a lot less bothered by people than their cousins the wood pigeons; is this because many of them are descended from inmates of dovecots in previous times, when they would be used to seeing humans up close?

May 4th

It's hard to tell which are the Sparrow-Cam fledgelings, but I can see several near the nestbox wing-flicking and being fed seeds, but also starting to look for their own food on the ground. They're able to fly, but not strongly. I wonder how Elvis is doing.

Bluetits have also bred in the garden without me even knowing they were nesting here. I can see a single fledgeling frantically flicking its wings and being fed by both parents, supplying aphids from the apple tree blossom. What has happened to the rest of the youngsters? Bluetits usually have a big brood.

The crows got a fledgling starling today.

May 5th

The Holly Blue aka Ivy Blue butterflies are evident today. I love how the life cycle of this exquisite small bright blue butterfly - feeding from both these sources during its life cycles - echoes the ancient celebrated connection between these two wonderful plant species. Both are key to the success of our particular garden: the holly provides the sparrows' top-rated roost and cover from predators, plus nectar blossom and then berries for birds; while the ivy also provides dense evergreen cover plus flowers and berries at times of year when these are rare, plus winter hosting for masses of invertebrates.

Numbers of this lovely little insect change greatly from year to year, thought to be on account of the varying effect of a highly specialised parasitic wasp for it is the only host. The butterflies have a spring brood and then a summer brood; what we're seeing today will be the tail end of the first brood, hanging around the holly, with the second coming in July or August, focusing on the ivy; in each case eating the flower buds, berries and small terminal leaves. Hence they're called after holly or ivy, but they're actually the exact same species. This is one of our few European butterflies that is generally on the increase, and extending northwards thanks to climate change.

May 6th

The male blackbird, not so very long ago warring even with his mate-to-be, is now calling his offspring to come down to the ground and even flicking his own wings. But the youngster seems too nervous to join him.

May 7th

There's been an ant's nest underneath the outside sill of our front door for a couple of years. Unusually today some of the ants are coming a little way into the house, which we want to discourage but in an eco-friendly way. I remember having been on retreat at a Buddhist monastery some decades ago where I noticed plenty of rabbits in the surrounding landscape but none coming in to eat plants in the unfenced vegetable garden. At the time I asked the abbot how this was achieved. "We simply ask them to eat just a little of our food plants," he said. The monks make this request as part of their daily meditation practice, and the rabbits comply. I'm going to try this.

May 8th

Excitement! Late yesterday evening when taking Rosa out for her bedtime walk we heard loud huffing, puffing and snorting in the garden, and saw that our big fat male hedgehog was on a date with a smaller hog, presumably female. This went on for a while, but for the time only seemed to comprise foreplay and much going round in circles.

The correct answer to the age-old joke 'How do hedgehogs make love?' is that the female can flatten down her prickles, though a modicum of care is no doubt still exercised. Offspring are usually born in June or July but a second litter can appear in late September or October. In this case the resultant progeny have much less chance of surviving the winter; this is why many of us look out for them in the colder months and either put food out for them or take them to a rescue centre if they really are too small and light.

But how to definitively tell the difference between male and female hedgehogs? The answer is that the male has a penile sheath in the middle of his abdomen, looking rather like a belly-button, and the penis is typically retracted into this. That is unless he is 'self-stimulating' - did you know that male hedgehogs self-stimulate? And just how do they do that? Carefully, one presumes.

Studies have shown that female hedgehogs prefer to use the gardens of semi-detached and terrace houses whereas males like to roam across the gardens of larger detached houses. This isn't an aesthetic preference; it's just that the bigger gardens carry more risk of encountering predators and the females rate safety more highly whereas the testosterone fuelled males are prepared to take more risk in order to find more mates.

Watching this courtship, Lord Byron's verse does indeed seem apposite:

"Let joy be unconfin'd
No sleep till morn, when youth and pleasure meet
To chase the glowing hours with flying feet!"

The unconfined joy is both theirs and mine.

May 9th

We're seeing the male wren again, bringing in nest material to the same site as before and calling from high branch tips nearby with his tail turned up high. Delighted to see this as we were wondering if he had departed. Does he still need to secure a mate, though?

We have a mixture of native bluebells (*Hyacinthoides non-scripts)* and the rival Spanish species *(H. hispanica)* in the garden; the latter were already here before we started rewilding, and we introduced a few of the native variety some years ago, bought from a reliable grower. Both have spread and are now in bloom. I'm struggling with the issue of whether to remove the Spaniards; they're notorious for being more vigorous, faster growing and able to cross-breed with the natives, creating fertile hybrids, and therefore likely take over in the long run.

The flowers of the Spanish conquistador bluebell, introduced three hundred years ago, are bigger, paler blue in colour and more erect, and lack the divine scent of the native variety. Primarily a woodland species, a bluebell colony takes five to seven years to develop.

The carrion crow came by today looking for eggs and fledglings, inspecting all the shrubs closely. I opened the window to scare him off but it didn't work, so I went outside and clapped at him, which worked. Leave my beloved ones alone!

May 10th

Keeping an eye on footage from the nocturnal trailcam. Continuing visits from assorted foxes, cats and our hedgehog, but not seeing the smaller hedgehog again so far. The hedgehog continues to alternate its visits through the night with presence of any fox.

The mystic/buddhistic ant request seems to be working.

Goldfinches are taking sheep's wool from the second empty suet cage; the one with Rosa's fur has long been emptied, but the sparrows had turned up their noses at this alternative. This must mean that they're onto a second brood.

May 11th

Love 'em or hate 'em, the wood pigeons represent a very successful species, so they must be doing something right – eating from diverse food sources and breeding for most of the year, for a start. Our resident male bird will go under the birdseed feeder when he sees the smaller birds eating there and hoover up the grains that fall as the others spill them. He'll be there every single day of the year that this food it provided but otherwise not be seen except when breeding.

A mate for him has now appeared. No doubt they will mate at all times of day and night, then make a token attempt at building a nest: just a few twigs across the forking branch in one of the taller shrubs. Then there's a fifty-fifty chance the eggs will fall out, in which case I can imagine the male cooing: "Oh dear, what a shame, now we're going to have to start mating all over again."

We humans have a whole clutch of expressions that help us identify and remember the calls of birds, with onomatopoeic phrasing that evoke the sounds and rhythms of their respective songs. There's "a little bit of bread and no cheese" for the yellowhammer; the chiffchaff call is characterised as "see-saw, see-saw", and the collared dove is said to sound like a football fan chanting, "U-ni-ted. U-ni-ted. U-ni-ted," whereas the woodpigeon's endlessly repetitive wheezing call with its funny little emphasis on certain bits sounds to me like nothing so much as "I *know* I'm boring! I *know* I'm boring", I *do* know I'm boring!" Perhaps male woodpigeons are competing in boringness, and females rejecting those who don't sound boring enough. It's certainly a species with a small range of samey and repetitive behaviour.

May 12th

The woodpigeon is not one of my favourite species, as you can tell – probably public enemy number four after magpies, crows and seagulls. Imagine my surprise today, then, when I find myself rescuing a young woodpigeon squab from two crows trying to tear it to bits, and looking like they're succeeding. When I intervene the crows move away and the squab flies to safety. It's either my epigenetic reflex to protect babies, or else I just want to disappoint the crows. Probably the latter. It works.

In the garden a starling fledgeling is being intermittently fed on the ground by a parent. When it's not being fed it pecks at the ground as it sees the adult doing, but doesn't know what it's looking for and so becomes disenchanted with that and approaches a sparrow instead and begs for food. Good luck with that.

The wren is perched on a high twig in full view of anyone who's looking, constantly bobbing and throwing its whole echo chamber of a body into its song which carries so well. They're such beautiful little birds with their russet brown colouring and paler bars. But they're essentially small brown birds that mostly hang out in dense vegetation and that's why they have such a loud, intricate and varied song.

May 13th

After assuming nothing would be happening with the SparrowCam nestbox since fledging, I took a random look today and was delighted to see five new eggs. There must be new incoming tenants and it has to be a new pair of sparrows as the first parents will have their hands full for a month or so. They must have moved in very quickly when it became available. Later in the day I see the two parents swapping roles and sitting on the eggs continuously, which means we could be some way down the road to hatching. What a great result for a new nestbox.

Slow-worms are now breeding in the compost heap: the ideal environment as it's warm, moist, sheltered and full of small creatures without a vertebra between them. They're oviparous meaning that there are eggs, but these hatch internally and the young are then born live: perfect miniatures of their parents, just a couple of inches long.

May 14th

The SparrowCam female is definitely talking to the eggs each time she settles down on them, in that special high pitched clucky voice. We know that nestlings of different species are affected by - and even learn - bird language before they hatch. There are still five eggs so it looks like that's their lot, with synchronised incubation already in motion and therefore synchronised hatching likely too.

Watching all these dedicated parents working non-stop through the days and nights makes you realise what a huge commitment and expenditure of resources is involved in bringing a family of young birds into the world. And there's always the risk that it could come to nothing if predators strike. The female in particular seems to hardly get to eat for much of the time. But for the sparrow flock as a whole the strategies are certainly paying off, with net increase in numbers year on year, while sparrows elsewhere are sadly in decline.

May 15th

Shock-horror-drama. I was taking Rosa on her bed-time walk last night when I saw two big seagull chicks walking along the pavement. At this time of year quite a few of these fall prematurely from their rooftop nests and then try to survive on the ground until they can fly. Next thing a fox rolls up; the gulls see it and retreat into a nearby garden; the fox follows them in. My instinct (despite seagulls' established 'public enemy' status) is to go in there and chase the fox away so that the gulls at least have a bit of life before they die; but I've got Rosa and I need to quickly tie her up. I do this – which takes about five seconds – and sprint into the garden. The two gulls are already dead and the fox hightails it over the wall. How did the fox do that in just about ten seconds? Remarkable. And ruthlessly efficient.

The parent birds are now looking round the street for these chicks. So that they will know that they're dead and not keep searching for them for days, I place the bodies where they can be easily seen. The fox will then be able to return and eat them later. Nature is indeed red in tooth and claw, as Tennyson memorably quipped - and foxes especially so.

May 16th

We've just seen a rat in the garden, and the neighbours have been seeing it in theirs regularly for a week – it's only there because they're putting bread on their bird table and some is knocked onto the ground by birds; seed doesn't attract rats. It's time for humane rat-trapping. Cheese is the chosen bait; the rat may think this choice clichéd but I'm sure will find it irresistible.

May 17th

We caught the rat (Brown or Norwegian rat, *Rattus Norvegicus*, which sounds made up but is its actual Latin name, like *Cattus*); it was really really angry. We released it at the riverside half a mile away and it scurried into the undergrowth. The riverbank is a good place for ratty to live.

The Brown Rat was accidentally introduced to Europe in the 1700s on ships from central Asia (not Norway, then) and travelled throughout the world, highly successful due to its adaptability and extraordinary breeding rate. It's an interesting, adaptable and intelligent creature; its ranks include a whole professional category called 'working rats'. These capable individuals work in forensics to sniff out gunshot residue and land mines as they're lighter, cheaper and easier to train than dogs. They can also be trained to lay computer cables through buildings; and make excellent service animals for people with disability. The oft-heard saying that in a city you're never more than six feet from a rat has been officially dismissed as bollox[1].

Humans need to be more like rats: more adaptable. In nature, the most successful wild species are those which are natural adaptors – like foxes, pigeons or the corvid family, whose populations remain steady when almost everything else is in decline. They change their food choices according to what is available, and their digestive systems have developed to cope with the variety. They change their food-finding patterns to whatever works. They change their behaviours when those become in-

1* *Footnote: Outraged readers may be disappointed to learn that the word bollox does not refer to male genitalia or indeed anything rude; it's actually an old Saxon word meaning nonsense or worthless information.*

effective or too risky. They have all evolved to be extremely wary of humans. But the ultimate change we as humans are asking species worldwide to adapt to is climate change; for very many, that's proving a step too far.

David Attenborough points out that seriously adapting the way we live on the Earth is the one thing that the human race as a whole needs to do. That's not just to save life on the planet; he suggests that continuing our current harmful interactions with wildlife could make global pandemics a frequent occurrence in the near future. We need to look after other species not just for their good but for our own. "In wildness is the salvation of the world" – thus spoke Henry David Thoreau, author of the classic text *Walden*, his classic reflection on simple living in natural surroundings.

May 18th

Another rat has now been seen and captured very quickly indeed – a smaller one, not so indignant at being trapped, and probably the hungry offspring of the first which must have been its mother. This one was duly taken to join mum on the riverbank, the trap re-set and almost immediately a third was captured. I suspect these two youngsters had been reliant on their mum for food. It's heart-warming, isn't it, when local social services authorities (me) can relocate a whole family together?

May 19th

Another not-yet-flying seagull chick tumbled into the street two days ago; this time I swung plan B into action before dusk would fall and any random fox could strike. I gathered it up and put it in a cardboard box; the parents didn't like this one little bit. I put the bird in Rosa's special yard at the back of our house, which foxes can't get into. The parents overhead could see where their baby was, and eventually calmed down. Rosa came out and started picking up on an interesting seagull smell, but as she is pretty much sightless now she just wandered round trying to find it and the bird just kept walking ahead of her. This went on for two days, with the parents watching at all times. By today the bird had learned to fly and left with mum and dad. Another success for social services.

May 20th

The SparrowCam female is sitting on the eggs continuously. I put bird seed down and the male immediately called to her from outside the nestbox, presumably telling her that food is available because she immediately popped out, whereupon he came in and sat on the eggs. Before long she returns and tells him she's taking over. I think she's found a keeper there in that partner. What with all this due diligence, and the talking to the eggs, it looks like hatching may start soon.

The joy of having a video nestbox positioned to be visible from where you're watching them on telly indoors is that you can see what they're doing outside just before they come in, and you can also tell what they're doing and where they're going immediately after they leave. That's the kind of obsessive detective work I enjoy.

May 21st

The bird bath is extremely popular in this heatwave weather, with birds queueing up for it. The male blackbird was in there first and then preened himself in the early morning sunshine – but he was constantly on the alert: one second of preening, then half a second of looking round: preen/ look/ repeat. He has a distinctive injury to the right wing which makes it droop, but that doesn't seem to affect his flying, his confidence or his ability to attract a mate.

The female blackbird continues to be comfortable in my presence and now their youngster is learning this behaviour too. Blackbirds are such attentive parents, making that soft clucking noise to quietly keep in touch with their young, but going straight into alarm call at the slightest sign of danger – usually a cat, around here.

May 22nd

SparrowCam hatching has begun, with three hatchlings today.

As darkness fell this particular evening I was surprised to see how late the wren kept hopping about, probably working overtime gathering insects for youngsters still in the undergrowth. The male blackbird was singing well into deep dusk, while the sparrows have been cosily tucked up in bed hours earlier. It seems like the single-unit families such as these two bird types have to work harder than the 'flock' species such as sparrow or starling.

Foraged foods from the garden this month have included nettle tops, wild carrot, three cornered garlic, dandelion flowers and Stickie Willie aka Goosegrass.

May 23rd

Four SparrowCam babies have now hatched.

It's nightingale season, so we venture out into the wider environment to hear those wonders. The best option in our vicinity has to be the Knepp estate, my spiritual/wildlife home-from-home for some years now. The estate has been running a large scale rewilding programme on the 3,500 acre ancestral estate farm. As well as species like deer deliberately brought in, threatened native species have introduced themselves because the environment is so hospitable, to the excitement of naturalists Europe-wide. This includes significant breeding numbers of cuckoos, turtle doves, nightingales, the magnificent purple emperor butterfly, and more.

As we travel to Knepp I'm reminded of our visits to the Bergerac region of France in past times when on dark summer nights I could hear three different nightingales singing at once from one listening spot. It's the males that sing, seeking to attract females which arrive later from southern climes. As each male finds a mate he stops singing and gets on with having a family. Nightingales are of course becoming increasingly rare nationally and internationally.

But Knepp turns out to be even more special. The hawthorn blossom is as profuse as I have ever seen it. In the evening sunshine we stand in one piece of recently self-naturalised scrubby woodland and listen; we hear simultaneously a nightingale, a cuckoo and – rarest of all – a turtle dove, the UK's fastest declining bird. What a treat.

May 24th

SparrowCam mum is still trying to hatch that last egg while dad is bringing in almost all of the takeaways. If one of them is going to be a serious runt then this would be a good start.

Some years ago I buried deciduous logs in the garden in the hope of attracting stag beetles, UK's largest beetle and another endangered species. We've recently seen males of the species flying in the vicinity on warm summer evenings; and today we've just spotted a female on the ground right inside the garden. The males fly in an ungainly way with their heavy bodies upright and wings out behind, making a loud droning buzz. They're often seen over roads because they're attracted to the residual evening heat of the tarmac. Their presence nearby means our female here is emitting pheromones that will be attracting their attentions.

It's generally only the male beetles that fly. These magnificent creatures can measure 7.5cm in length and have fearsome looking antlers, which are there to impress females and to fight males; it's thought that these antlers actually prevent the males from feeding on the tree sap they would otherwise eat, so they don't live very long from maturity. The female is considerably smaller and doesn't have the antlers.

Tidying up dead wood is bad for stag beetles, and that's being done a lot these days. It's all about leaving decaying wood underground for the female to lay up to twenty-one eggs within. When the eggs hatch into fat white larvae with orange heads they spend from three to seven years eating before emerging as adults. Their adult life is extremely short: the males mate and die, and the females lay eggs and die; so you would hope their larval stage is a lot of fun. And that they enjoy staying in one spot and eating, because that's all they do.

This is another gratifying sign that measures taken in the garden eventually produce results. As they say in the movies, 'if you build it, they will come' - but they may well take their time.

May 25th

The local starling flock, who visit the garden but don't live in it, seem to be having a particularly good breeding season too. All the adults seem to have more than one teenager to look after - which would be a magnet for predators - so they're frequently taking advantage of this protected space that's so full of food and hard to see into from the outside. Today the youngsters are learning for the first time how to drink water from the birdbath by closely watching their parents and trying to follow suit. When they approach the water for the first time they think it's going to be food and seem disappointed, but soon realise that water is essential too. Presumably up to now they've obtained water from the juicy insects they're being fed, so this is another step towards self-catering.

May 26th

Both male and female blackbird parents are in the apple tree with beaks full of insects, looking round for their young to join them, but none are appearing. An adolescent starling recognises this behaviour and approaches them with high hopes - but it's no deal.

May 27th

We've seen three collared doves flying together down the street, which we think are the attentive parents and the wayward youth we rescued from the road recently. The one in our own garden has now fledged and is being fed there.

May 28th

The last SparrowCam egg is clearly not going to hatch so mum has finally given up on brooding it. It's been interesting to see how long she continued with that. The other four are growing apace.

May 31st

I do wonder about my confessed habit of distinguishing between 'public enemy' and 'preferred friend' species; I guess I just want things to match my personal tastes and preferences. But isn't letting a garden go wild an odd thing a person with such a disposition to do? Shouldn't wild gardening be all about letting things take their course: laissez-faire gardening? It's a philosophical dilemma.

But here's the thing: a teensy weensy bit of intervention can make the garden work for wildlife all the better - a bit of supplementary feeding, an occasional touch of foliage control, building a wee pond. The pond in particular has increased the perceived value of the territory to resident creatures and attracted more of them - providing drinking and bathing water for birds, mammals and insects, providing habitat for amphibians and for water invertebrates, increasing biodiversity with water plants. But does this let me off the discriminatory hook? Probably not.

Freaque du control, moi? You have no idea.

June

June 1st

In the garden the breeding season continues and life is rich as ever. The surviving baby sparrows in the flock are now big fat fledglings, fully feathered and flying well, able to find their own food, but many are still chasing their slim mothers around, demanding feeding and calling incessantly. These particular youngsters are now identifiable from their plumage as males; you can tell that the mums know they're taking the p**s and can clearly feed themselves, because they're universally ignoring these demands. I suppose you could call it *man-fledging*; the female fledglings don't do it.

June 2nd

Many birders and twitchers haven't much time for the birds they see most often and only rate the rarer sightings; I'm the opposite, as you can probably tell. My big favourites are the sparrows – here in this confined garden we can see deeply into how they live, how they interact, what motivates them and what dramas they enact. I also specially appreciate the blackbirds, which we also see a lot of up close in this garden through the year.

There are now two male blackbirds co-existing in the garden so I'm presuming they've got to be father and son; there's no way another male would be tolerated. This means the second bird is a youngster but is displaying adult male colouring. It looks like the dad must be showing his son where to find what kind of food, and the son is now learning for himself rather than begging to be fed. But once that process is fully learned he'll be sent packing to find his own territory.

This father has a drooping right wing, probably the result of injury in a fight with another male or attack by unsuccessful predator. It's a helpful identifier as it's always difficult with blackbirds to tell whether you've got the same or changing individuals.

Seeing the father doing the feeding usually means the female - the friendly one with the damaged tail feather - is preparing for the next nesting attempt, of which there can be up to four in a season. Fledglings from the last brood of the season will then be fed jointly by both parents. Their dedication and parenting skills fill me with admiration. And of course the song is out of this world.

I'm also disproportionately fond of wrens. Today I see again the bright russet coloured specimen closely chasing a slightly duller coloured one round the lower hedges in the garden.

June 3rd

I'm keeping an eye on the wrens spotted yesterday, and today have located a nest site. It only occurred because we were sitting in the garden when dusk fell; the only birds about at that time were

the wrens and I noticed two different birds disappearing repeatedly into the same dense area of foliage. With this frequency of visiting there must be young to feed, and they have be growing fast as these two birds were kept busy finding food until late.

June 4th

Another first in this garden, and a particular rarity in urban environments: a Summer Chafer lands on my hand while I meditate outside. I thought it was the regular Cockchafer, took a photo and posted it on Facebook where people joked that I just wanted an excuse to use the two components of this word in public. But another commenter put me right about the species, which is smaller than its near relative. The colour is beautiful burnished bronze ranging to gold and I adore it. Both varieties are ungainly flying insects which often bump into people in their search for a mate in the early summer months.

June 5th

The Ivy Blues are laying eggs on the underside of ivy leaves in early evening twilight - a good move as most birds will have stopped feeding by then.

Our street's WhatsApp group is abuzz this morning with word of a young crow wandering around the street, having fallen out of the tree the parents are nesting in. Can someone help?

I wander down purely out of curiosity. This one is definitely not going to be able to fly very soon: its primary wing feathers have not grown out of their sheaths. It's quite common for young crows to have two or three flightless days out of the nest before being able to fly, but everyone is worried that this one will be run over by a car or eaten by foxes tonight. I can't quite believe I do this – crows are my public enemy #2 - but I get big gloves and succeed in catching it, whereupon all hell breaks loose from the parents who are watching closely. The raucous protesters are joined by a third adult - last year's young? one of the in-laws? – who is equally indignant. It can't be baby cuteness and genetic proto-parental programming that persuaded me to do this: there's nothing cute about this large and formidable uber-fledgling.

Baby Crow isn't the least bit happy either about being grabbed; it keeps squirming and trying to stab me with its sharp beak, but I manage to keep out of reach of that. I place the bird in the crown of a tree but within seconds it's on the ground again. A neighbour shoos it into her back garden where she thinks it will be safer and where she can keep an eye on it. This young crow becomes the WhatsApp group's soap-opera star of the day, christened Precocious Crow, and will probably continue in the role for some days.

June 6th

Precocious Crow updates, commentaries and well-intentioned advice are all over the WhatsApp group this morning. The hosting neighbour reports that PC has survived the night and gobbled chips put out for it. The three adult crows are now camped in the trees in her garden.

In other news, solitary bumble bees are feeding in numbers on the flowering jasmine. I'm still eating foraged nettle tops – a terrific source of iron and good for strengthening and detoxifying the blood, reducing inflammations, and supplying vitamins A, C and D. When I was growing up in Ireland we'd see older country folk deliberately stinging their hands with them to treat arthritis; the ancient Egyptians knew about this too. Nettles are great to have in the garden as food for ladybirds and a variety of moths and butterflies including the lovely tortoise-shell but they can take over if you let them.

June 7th

Precocious Crow is now able to hop some way off the ground - though not yet able to fly - so has moved to a perch out of reach of cats. If I were a cat I'd stay away from this one. But foxes are still a danger by night.

June 8th

Early this morning Precocious Crow had gone, and so had the parental vigilante group. No-one knows whether it was able to fly off or whether the foxes got it. My money is on the latter; I know how efficient they are.

I went for a short walk wearing the same hat as I wore when 'rescuing' P.C., and the crows went berserk again. So now at least I've discovered a sure-fire way of disrupting them if they're in the garden doing something I don't like: I'll wear that hat. And crows have a long and detailed memory. Whatever I feel about these creatures, they certainly take their parenting seriously.

A baby squirrel is on its own in the garden, no sign of the other twin. This one is not growing very quickly at all.

June 9th

I look out my bedroom window and see a male sparrow-hawk – much the smaller of the pair - perched on the highest shrub.

Perching like this means he's not hunting right now and isn't worried about being seen; he's probably launched an unsuccessful attack and is now catching his breath. If the hunt had been successful he'd have the prey in his talons or be far away with it. Female birds of prey are nearly always larger than their mates; is this so that they can stop the male from eating the young if food became desperately short? Or is it so they can lay the large eggs involved?

I'm prone to pondering on such things. I also wonder why I'm prejudiced against magpies but not sparrow-hawks. Is that because the hawks tend to take birds that are weaker or less alert, leaving the strongest and most capable behind and do a decent day's work for each kill, whereas magpies will find a source of fledglings and come back until there all eaten? And because magpie numbers are spiralling out of control? Probably not; Spockians would say I'm driven entirely by illogical emotion.

On the plus side, it turns into a wonderful warm evening and stag beetles are on the wing again. They're now flying in over our high surrounding shrubs and crash-landing in the garden; our female must be weaving her pheremonetastic spell. And the wild strawberries are ripe too. What's not to like?

June 10th

The second lot of SparrowCam nestlings is fledging; two have gone today. One of the two remaining is so much smaller than its sibling that it snuggles underneath it as if it were a parent.

June 11th

One of the last two SparrowCam youngsters has now fledged, leaving one plus the single egg, with one parent still doing food deliveries.

June 12th

Last SparrowCam nestling finally fledges. I hope it survives as it's rather underdeveloped.

And it looks like the hawk came back and made a kill – there's that characteristic sparrow- hawk's perfectly-spread-out circle of sparrow feathers, which means the prey was plucked before being taken away to feed the mate or the young at the nest site. No way of telling which sparrow or fledgeling was the victim.

The sparrows' consistent breeding success in this garden isn't only good for the sparrows; it's good for other species too, like this hawk or the magpies and the crows. But other smaller birds benefit too from the sparrows' presence; the latter's behaviour is reassuring for bluetits, goldfinches and others wondering whether it's safe to be out and about; the sparrow flock furnishes an excellent early warning system with so many eyes keeping a lookout. They're all going to be jittery for a day or two now.

June 13th

A pair of bluetits is feeding on the early shift this morning, ahead of sparrow rush-hour. They use the seed feeder differently from the sparrows; they dive in, grab a seed, fly to a nearby branch to eat it, and keep doing that as long as the coast is clear. The sparrows by contrast cling on to the feeder and eat until they're pushed off by another sparrow.

Surprising, then, that these two little birds have a territory of which this garden is just a part, while a whole sparrow flock can manage with just this garden. But then they do bully all the other small birds off the food.

June 14th

The woodpigeons are looking for nesting materials again; looks like the last nest failed to contain their eggs; they're also looking for a different site. I notice the female sitting in the middle of the densest shrub we have: a hawthorn thoroughly interwoven with honeysuckle. It's the sparrows' most consistent and longest established roosting site.

June 15th

The hen woodpigeon is still sitting in the hawthorn tree. I'm pretty sure she's bagging it as a nesting site and I'm not happy about that. Woodpigeons are somewhere on the public enemy list and therefore have limited citizen's rights, while sparrows are at the top of the preferred species list. The reason I'm concerned is that these birds constantly crash about having noisy sex in the middle of the night; that's going to interrupt my beloved sparrows' beauty sleep and maybe chase them out of their roost altogether. I'm not going to let that happen; am considering what to do. Does this make me prudish? I don't care.

Last thing in the evening, I step out into the garden. There's no Mr HH, but to my delight I see a small bat flying round the street lamp outside the house, catching night flying insects attracted by the light. Last year I put up a bat box and this is the first sighting; maybe it's living there. It looks like a Pipistrelle and flies like a big dark moth. What a joy it is to see in this urban setting; having a bat present is an indicator of healthy insect numbers and other environmental factors.

June 16th

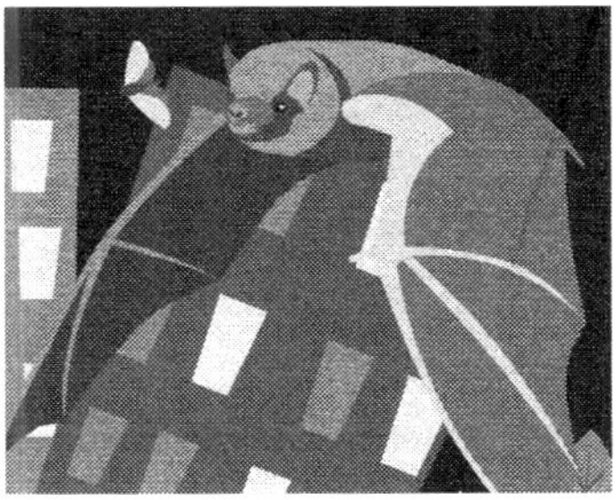

The female wood pigeon is still spending time sitting in the hawthorn; something has to be done. I have a plan. Armed with a broom, I sneak up and stand underneath the tree, from which position I can look up and see her from below, sitting cosily underneath the top canopy and dozing happily with her head tucked into her chest. Wood pigeons are nervous birds, but what threat could there possibly be to her, she must be thinking, when she's safely ensconced under this almost impenetrable cover? So her guard is completely switched off. I turn the broom around so the handle is upwards and slowly thread it upwards through the undergrowth until it's just below her. Imagine her surprise when I gently poke the underside of her body; she explodes upwards and out of the tree. I think I've convinced her that this is not a safe nesting site for pigeons. Result!

Does this treatment of a wild animal make me a bad person? Probably so.

June 17th

Goldfinches are feeding at the sow thistle flower heads, separating the thistledown from the seed so that it drifts away continuously in the breeze. No other birds have a finely pointed enough beak to extract the fine seeds from plants like thistle and teasel. You can feed goldfinches on sunflower seed hearts or on Nyjer seeds from a special feeder with very narrow feeding slots, but I reckon naturally grown and seasonal native produce is going to be better for them. The sow thistle is a plant I eat the leaves of too.

Later I see a young goldfinch sitting in the apple tree and wing-flicking like mad with the parent bird hopping all around it, finding insects under the apple leaves and taking them to the fledgling. Unlike the sparrows, these chicks don't advertise their presence by incessant chirping. It's great to see these youngsters; it means the birds have managed to build a new and more successful nest than the one that got blown away earlier in the year.

June 18th

On the street outside our gate today I see the two local carrion crows attack a baby magpie which is doesn't stand a chance against these two. It's raising mixed feelings for me. These two species are mortal enemies; almost immediately six adult magpies appear from nowhere and wade in, and there's a big punch-up. When they see me watching the whole assembly takes to the tree overhead and there continue yelling and shrieking at one another for the rest of the morning. Never a dull moment.

I have to say that the pair of crows has done an excellent job this spring in keeping the magpies preoccupied in protecting their own young rather than grabbing fledgeling sparrows and other species inside our garden, which has happened more in previous years.

June 19th

Three sparrows are sitting in the apple tree. One is a big fat fledgling flicking its wings like mad. As soon as one of the adult birds moves to a new position the BFF hops next to it and begs for food. It's not getting any; the message is clear: Find your own ****ing food - you're big enough now.

We used to get a lot of aphids on the fruit trees and other plants in this garden, as well as apple and also plum codling moths. But since it became established as a wild garden these problems have disappeared and we don't need to treat for these moths. Ladybirds, hoverflies, sparrows and bluetits seem to keep them under control; indeed, the aphids become a valuable resource rather than a gardener's problem.

June 20th

A third sparrow couple has moved into the SparrowCam nest-box - and there are already four more eggs. That's extraordinary for a new unit, only put up in March.

June 21st

Starlings celebrate the summer solstice. When the sun is at its highest a flock of thirty of them has chosen the tops of the lower shrubs in the garden – relatively hidden from predators by the higher hedging trees – to drape themselves out with wings outstretched, basking in the UV light which kills the feather mites with which all birds that live in close proximity to one another are plagued. Starlings' summer sunbeds!

June 22nd

The sparrows in general are already mating again, the favoured location for assignations being in the rainwater gutters. Late second and early third broods will be coming up soon. The blackbirds may have another brood already; I can see the hen bird bringing food into the tangle of thorny pyracanthas and honeysuckle.

June 23rd

Honeysuckle is growing through almost all the shrubs in the garden and it's now emitting a heavenly scent in the still air both day and night. Food in quantity is being brought into their nest-site area by the blackbirds. I watch the hen bird smashing a snail, shaking it and scraping off as much shell as possible. She doesn't seem bothered that I will know where the nest is - after all, she's the female I rescued and who has befriended me ever since. Meanwhile I can hear the male singing from a high point nearby; I guess that's what he sees as his contribution at present.

June 25th

Today I see Drooping Wing Blackbird fly up, pull a snail from the house gutter, fly back down and bash it about on the ground, as the female did the other day.

June 26th

DWB is now diligently finding snails and bringing them to the nest; not bad going for during daytime, when self respecting snails will be hiding in deep cover. Not just a pretty singer then.

June 27th

DWB's snailfest continues; this seems to be the fledgling's only food choice at present. He's still being meticulous about taking time to bash off shell fragments from each one; obviously doesn't want any nestling choking on those. After snail hunting for a while he gets back to singing from a high spot, then more snailing, and so on; he does this all day. Is his singing intended to deter rival males from muscling in on the territory? His singing perch during the day is right over the nest rather than on the house chimney pot or television aerial which are the loftiest points available, but which he now only uses for his first and last songs of the day. Every time it rains he stops singing, but doesn't stop hunting cochleoids. I'm not seeing the hen bird at the moment; maybe she can stay with the young as he's bringing so much food. I can imagine the conversation at the nest: "Not snails again, Mum!" .... "Come on children, eat up your snails or you won't get your worms for pudding."

June 28th

The third set of SparrowCam eggs has suddenly and mysteriously been abandoned. Why? Has there been predation of one parent or even both? A single parent bird will have a poor chance of both incubating eggs and getting food, and when fledging time comes things will be even more difficult, so a singleton will often decide to abandon, especially if male. The other possible explanation could be that the nest has become unacceptably infested with feather mites or other parasites. The parents birds can eventually decide these are too unbearable and too unhealthy for them, and would also reduce the chances of survival for any young. Sometimes in the lives of wild creatures the hard but best decision is that it's not worth investing energy to continue, better to start again while there are still good breeding conditions. Either way, we'll make sure we remove all bedding and disinfect the nestbox during the winter.

June 29th

A bumblebee has made a nest under the stone in the garden on top of which sits a Buddha statue. A tortoiseshell butterfly is basking in early morning sunshine. It's idyllic in the garden in many ways. But any time the crows see me and I'm wearing that hat they still recognise me and yell, "You're the one who stole our ******* baby!" I reckon crows swear a lot.

Interfering busybody, moi? Absulutement.

Thanks to Ruth Stevens for sponsorship of the June illustrations.

July

July 1st

Breeding in the garden is becoming slightly less frenetic. Weather is relatively cool but dry. Drooping Wing Blackbird is feeding snails to a hidden entity away from the nest area; does this mean fledging of brood number two has begun?

July 2nd

We're seeing the new blackbird fledgling today. It's mostly being fed in the foliage but sometimes follows DWB on the ground, flicking its wings to ask for food; what I'm hearing is 'Can you find something different from snails, Dad?' Haven't seen mum yet – maybe she's looking after another youngster. Blackbird eggs are usually laid one each morning, and the hen doesn't sit on them – which starts the hatching process - until all are laid; this is so they will hatch and develop simultaneously to make protection and provisioning easier. At that early stage it can look as if the nest has been abandoned because the hen is deliberately not sitting on them until all are laid so that they will all grow at the same rate. This is in contrast to the many larger birds, especially birds of prey, which start sitting on eggs as soon as they are laid, with eggs often days apart. In this case they're investing most heavily in the first hatchers so that they will have at least one young raised, and if there isn't enough food then only the smaller hatchlings - in which there has been less investment - will be lost. In cases of extreme shortage of prey food, the smaller hatchlings may be eaten by - or fed - to the larger.

Blackbird fledglings can't fly for an unusually long time so they stay hidden in cover until they can safely hop down to the ground and fly well. This is why the nests are usually in relatively low positions.

It's also possible that there's only one fledgling; when all fledging has been done the female will usually start preparing the nest for the next lot and leave feeding mainly to the male, and that may be what she is doing right now.

Later in the day I see the male preparing another snail, and next thing both he and the youngster are under cover; then I understand why; I see a lurking magpie keeping a watch on them. DWB flies down to the ground again on his own, and as he lands his tail is up in defiance; maybe this is a signal to the youngster that there's danger about. He's preparing a number of snails now; one of the benefits of this garden is that there are plenty of these hidden in the edges of the ground foliage even during a drought. Blackbird fledglings need plenty of such soft food as snails, slugs and caterpillars. Even if they might prefer worms.

July 3rd

The sparrows continue to be extremely vociferous even though the breeding cycle has reached a less frenzied stage. There do appear to be more of them than in early spring, so breeding seems to have been successful again despite much predation.

July 5th

In the garden both apples and plums are swelling now in good numbers, showing no ill effect from the dry spring and early summer weather: once again demonstrating the moderating effects of a mature wild garden. The sparrows are knocking some of the smaller apples off the tree, presumably looking for insects.

Two robins on the apple tree are bobbing and tail-raising. It looks like courtship but something isn't quite right; it's going on for ages and they're not facing towards each other, but both keep looking towards the hedge.

July 6th

One of the two robins I saw yesterday has gone but the other is still sitting out in the open, incessantly bobbing up and down and tipping its tail up. It's now got a caterpillar in its beak and looks like it's trying to capture the attention of another bird.

After fifteen minutes the robin gives up, hops down into low foliage and reappears a minute later without the caterpillar. Is it feeding a fledgling in there?

But then I see another robin doing the same procedure, but this time it flies in to the nest site which I've worked out is about a metre off the ground, deep in a very dense patch of jasmine; you can see absolutely nothing from the outside. Does this mean there are fledglings at different stages, one on the ground and others still in the nest? This is the stuff of wild gardening detective work and I love it.

July 7th

In early sunshine three kinds of butterfly are nectaring in the garden's central area, which more and more resembles a forest glade: Peacock, Meadow Brown and Cabbage White - even though there are no cabbages anywhere near here.

A single robin is still finding food, flying into the apple tree facing the nest, bobbing and tail-tipping, but still nobody's coming out to take it.

July 8th

Some sparrows are gathering nest materials again for yet another brood.

I'm still seeing that single male robin and he's still trying to get youngsters to come out for food but now seems more excitable and is moving from perch to perch, always looking towards where the nest is. But in the end he has to once more fly right into the nest site with the food.

Robins are usually ultra secretive about where there nest is located, and I know this one is aware that I'm watching because he's also turning his head to look at me a lot. I believe he's the one that got accustomed to seeing me putting out food and joining me when I'm doing garden work.

It looks like the young must all be fledged by now, but still not keen to leave the site and fly into the open.

July 9th

Robin still offering food but with no takers in the open; but he's not doing it at such short intervals now. Robins are very attentive parents, and will often feed nestlings or fledgelings of other small bird species.

A variety of solitary species of bumblebees is all over the lavender which is blooming in the garden's sunniest spot; it's a magnet for pollinators. This always lifts my spirits. At other times on these blossoms we see honey bees, hoverflies and various butterflies. Odd fact: dried lavender flowers are used as an insect repellent. Isn't nature surprising?

July 10th

Another change on the robin front: both parents are now flying in to the nest site. Could I be seeing more than two robins? Probably not, they'd be nesting too close to one another to be acceptable to either.

July 11th

Finally, after six days of parental coaxing all robins have disappeared. I guess they've finally become confident flyers and the parents have taken them off. A success story, then, and another example of patient and dedicated parenting.

This stuff reminds me once again how much being close to wild nature helps with our emotional and mental wellbeing. Society is beginning to wake up to the fact, and science is backing it up.

Research is also showing that having just a small patch of wild nature around you, such as in a wild urban garden, brings the same benefit.

The word *ecopsychology* was coined in 1992 to describe the study of the mental health benefits of being in nature, and as the years pass it's being taken more and more seriously. Richard Louv coined the term *nature-deficit disorder* in 2005 and identified it as a cause of many ills including depression, hyper-stress and lack of creativity.

Our minds are affected by the modern world; urban living causes our sympathetic nervous system, controlling the well-known fight-or-flight response, to be on constant high alert causing constant stress and associated problems like anxiety, depression, high blood pressure and heart disease.

But as the vast majority of our evolutionary development took place in a completely natural world, our unnatural modern setting can produce a big disconnect with those elements we need for our wellbeing, elements we evolved to need around us and to function well in. From an evolutionary point of view we're still basically outdoor animals. Being in touch with the wild can reawaken those ancient instincts and intuitions which we needed to survive in prehistoric times – to get something to eat and to avoid being eaten, and to experience a meaningful, satisfying and joyful life in the presence of wildness. Being in touch with nature calms our nervous systems. This is why wilding and rewilding of the spaces close to where we live near can be so powerful and transformative.

Today many different authorities– including conservation organisations, healthcare professionals and even national governments– are going further and recognising that connecting with nature and spending time in the natural environment is a significant medical resource that can be methodically tapped into, in order to help with mental ailments as well as to top up emotional wellbeing. David Strayer at the department of psychology, University of Utah shows from research there that "There are increased benefits from spending more time in nature and leaving technology behind – such as enhanced memory, better problem solving ability, greater creativity, lower levels of stress, and higher feelings of positive wellbeing."

Walking in nature is now prescribed by doctors in UK's NHS for conditions ranging from anxiety and depression to diabetes and high blood pressure, even if it's just taking a walk in a local park. A recent study by Exeter University has shown that just two hours of time spent in nature per week produces measurable benefits of this sort; that's just 15 to 20 minutes a day. It's also becoming recognised that there will be material gains too at the macro level: less cost to health services, fewer medications needed, less time taken off work from sickness.

A study survey of 26,000 people in 26 European countries published by the German Centre for Integrative Biodiversity Research is even more interesting in the context of the potential for gardens. It demonstrates that being in the vicinity of bird diversity brings quantifiable increases in happiness and that conservation is as important to human wellbeing as financial security. It found that the happiest Europeans are those living in near-natural surroundings that are home to diverse wild creatures: in other words, a wilded garden. It further concluded that enticing fourteen additional bird species to your environment brings the individual as much satisfaction as earning an additional $150 per month. What's not to like about that?

If you live in the city, it's going to be difficult to get into nature every day – unless you have it there in your even partly wilded urban garden. Rachel Kaplan of the department of Psychology at the University of Michigan reports: "People don't have to head for the woods to enjoy nature's restorative effects. Even a glimpse of nature from a window helps."

July 12th

Three blackbirds are in the open in the garden together today: mum, dad and baby. Dad is taking a birdbath so baby tries to get fed by flying to mum. Mum doesn't comply. Dad flies down to the ground and baby hops over to him for food. No deal from dad either. They must be weaning their stay-at-home teenager off dependency on bank of mum and dad.

July 13th

Most of the sparrows now have another brood hatching, probably mostly third or fourth batches; these industrious little wonders don't hang about.

July 14th

The vigilante crows are now recognising me without the hat, their yelled abuse now roughly translating as "That's the **** that ****** took our ****** baby!!!" Their language is getting worse.

Plums are beginning to ripen on the tree. It's always the same branch that has the first ripe plum; it must get the most favourable combination of protection and sunlight. The tree produces succulent plums of a type I've never seen in a shop, but not many of them. We pick them off, one at a time, just as they ripen perfectly and just before the birds get to them and divide each one between the two of us to savour its deliciousness.

A few years ago the tree sprouted a sucker from its base below the rootstock and this has now grown into another tree. It's highly likely to revert to a different plum variety, the one that our tree was grafted onto. Now there are some fruits forming for the first time, so this year we'll see what these new plums are like. The new tree has grown vigorously, which is typical for the rootstock, and is now taller than the old one; the first small fruits have appeared on the single lowest branch, with a lot of them packed in close together.

July 15th

The male blackbird started singing at 4.10 this morning: it's beautiful and uplifting as ever. This is perhaps these islands' most popular singing bird, given that it's very widespread and fits in well with many people's lives. I know this bird is probably saying, "This is my territory so don't even think about coming into my space or you'll seriously regret it" but I never fail to feel joy from listening to it, especially just before dawn and again at dusk. Who knows, perhaps the bird feels joy too: maybe the joy of telling others to **** off? That's something I often enjoy.

Before long, though, the gulls nesting on a nearby rooftop start up their raucous outraged din and the blackbird stops. It's another hour before the sparrows even wake up; I wonder if these late sleepers complain to one another about the gulls disturbing their slumber, as most humans here do? They certainly like their lie-in; I'm wondering if they can get away with this because they know their flock holds this permanent territory, whereas the non-flocking species such as blackbird and robin have to keep reasserting their rights from the earliest hour?

July 16th

The blackbird fledgling – I'm still only seeing one from this current brood – is out in the open now, waiting to be fed by DWB and at the same time starting to look for food of its own, but not very effectively. It's plumage is speckled brown so I'm not sure of its gender as yet.

July 17th

Stop press, there's another fledgling blackbird. The two of them are sitting together right on my upstairs office windowsill, waiting to be fed. It's great to see them so close up.

July 18th

DWB is sunbathing today, lying sprawled on the ground with wings completely outspread out, to kill external parasites such as lice with the combination of heat and UV rays just as the starlings were doing on the shrub tops. The presence of feather lice isn't just a hygiene issue; too many of them can weaken the bird and make the plumage duller and less attractive to mates. If the sunlight doesn't kill the lice straight off, it can at least cause them to move to less entrenched positions where they may then be removed by preening. This is birds' main reason for preening, though it also helps get their feathers all settled in the right position after flying, bathing or having a scrap.

DWB must be confident there are no predators about or he wouldn't be doing this. The garden is certainly hard to see down into with the high surrounding hedging.

July 19th

I've been enjoying observation of the local starlings; they don't come into the garden much - unless I've put a suet block up whereupon they appear instantly as if by magic and decimate it in seconds – but in the mornings and towards dusk I see them congregate on the tree outside our gate for their daily commute to and from the local mass murmuration which is not many miles away.

I love the calls starlings make when they're gathered in numbers like this. They have an extraordinary range of vocal effects – which is thought to be needed because they don't hold territories as most songbirds do, and because the males have to compete against many others close at hand in the flock - and are excellent mimics. They can whistle, chatter, warble, whir, scream, and make harsh rattles and trills; and they can imitate many other birds including birds of prey; a skill they may have developed so they can use it to discourage other smaller bird species and so avoid sharing a food source with them. This is another evolutionary reason why starlings have developed the ability to imitate other sounds as part of ability to imitate other birds' calls, and they've done that because in the mating season females select mates that can perform the longest song with the greatest range of different components.

Starlings also use these calls variously to communicate their whereabouts, express aggression or other reactions, and to warn of danger. One of my favourite calls of theirs is the very particular sound they make when the sun is shining and they seem happy because they're taking time to just sit there and sing: it's a single extended note that swoops down from high to lower pitch. You'll hear it a lot if you walk down many streets in sunny weather. They can also make all kinds of un-bird-like noises, imitating anything they hear regularly from mobile phone ringtones to pneumatic drills. They're a close relative of the minah bird, one of nature's greatest mimics.

Numbers on this daily starling commute reduce, of course, during the breeding season when the breeding pairs stay at their nests all day, and then increase when northern European starlings move here during the winter months, which is why the most spectacular murmurations occur then.

July 20th

DWB is feeding a greedy fledgeling on the apple tree with large beakfuls of white stuff. Is it cabbage white butterflies, or white bread from a neighbour's garden? This fledgeling is now the same size or maybe a little bigger than dad; surely it should be finding its own food by now?

Watching the sparrows go to their roost in the late afternoon, I wonder: how do roosting birds not fall off their perches when they sleep? It's because of a specialised design feature: as they relax into slumber their weight bearing down through their legs automatically locks their toes around the branch they're perching on; so they don't need to keep exerting pressure. Might this continue to function if they died in their sleep? Would then they just stay on the perch till they decomposed? These are the sort of things I need to know on a need-to-know basis.

July 21st

The garden delivers continuing wonders. In the evening something special is happening at the ants' nest just outside our door, which is usually very quiet. But today, they've decided, is Flying Ant Day. On this day, just once a year, virgin female queens and great numbers of flying male workers leave their nest on nuptial flights to mate and then set up new colonies; the mated females descend to Earth, pull off their wings, and search for a nest site to set up a new colony. This is always undertaken when the conditions are just right: when a spell of wet weather is followed by warm, humid and windless conditions. The flying ants can be so numerous and so synchronised over large parts of the country, with swarms up to fifty miles across, that the UK Meterological Office's radar sometimes mistakes them for rain clouds.

The sparrows have not failed to notice this bounty and are having a bonanza, some catching the winged ants in the air while others eat them on the ground before they've taken off. It's carnage, but the ants are so numerous that most are escaping.

When I look up and down the street, I can see exactly the same thing happening all over the neighbourhood, with flying ants emerging from huge numbers of tiny holes in pavements and the footings of walls as well as from people's gardens, where you never knew there were ants' nests in the first place. Out here the starlings and seagulls have cottoned on too, walking over the ground to catch them and also catching them high overhead. It's quite a sight.

I love this occasion; it fills me with wonder at the amazingness and potential richness of wild life, and with happiness that things like this can still happen in our urban settings. It's our local zero-budget version of those epic TV Blue-Planet style feeding frenzies you see on TV, where a massive shoal of fish is caught between attacks by tuna, gannets, dolphins and blue whales.

Online this evening, however, I see that many people have been freaked out by this phenomenon, as if they were being invaded by swarms of locusts. Indeed many people hate ants all year round; it's that terrible attitude again, that nature is a danger and must be extinguished, so out with the toxic sprays and chemicals. But these creatures are completely harmless; in a couple of hours they will have completely disappeared, with fallen bodies soon hoovered up by birds, mice, hedgehogs and other creatures who won't be able to believe their good fortune.

Ants really are amazing. Merlin Sheldrake mentions that in 2011 termite ants got into an Indian bank and ate ten million rupees worth of notes. And now we today we are seeing many billions of ants over large areas of England all managing to pick exactly the same day - and the same part of that day - for this fledging event. How do they do this? It's another of nature's miracles. Some day we'll know how, but in the meantime let's just experience the wonder. Ants are just one tiny fraction of the incredible diversity and complexity that exists in the natural world, but encountering them in the wildlife garden helps me connect and be inspired by it all.

July 22nd

I'm surprised by the appearance of one of the baby squirrels on my office windowsill where it has taken to sitting and looking in at me. Much as I disapprove of grey squirrels, it's undeniably cute and surprisingly tame. Its mum having been taken away when the twins were still in the dray, it seems never to have learned to be as fanatically wary of humans as its parent would have taught it to be. Maybe when it's an adult, if it survives till next spring, it will not have learned to eat birds' eggs and young. It looks just about halfway to full size now, completely white on its underside.

To tell the truth, I'm full of admiration for this creature's survival thus far without parental support. I can tell it's hungry because it's nibbling at the pebbledash rendering on the outside wall; I'm not sure how much nutritional value it'll get from that. Is it giving me a hint? Does it know about those peanuts I have stashed away to feed the bluetits? Or is it trying to persuade me to re-evaluate my views on grey squirrels? Either way, it's certainly hanging round on these visits to the windowsill and I'm enjoying its company.

July 23rd

Bumblebees are still flying in and out of the nest under the big stone in the garden underneath the statue of the Buddha. I wonder if these benign vibes played a part in their queen choosing this site?

Now I'm seeing two baby squirrels.

July 25th

The tree with ripening plums is a big focus for the sparrows again; they don't eat the fruit - though starlings and others do - so I presume they're finding sugar-loving insects there and thus helping protect the fruit. It's the least they could do, as they were most likely responsible for how few plums there are now; in spring they attacked the flowers like nobody's business.

July 27th

Sitting in the garden in sunlight, a tiny grasshopper-like insect lands on my hand. It measures less than a millimetre in body length and has antennae three or four times that length. I take a macro photo and put it on Facebook for identification. Turns out it's a Speckled Bush Cricket, a first for this garden. I never knew crickets could be so small. I learn that the only distinction between grasshoppers and crickets is that the latter walk away from danger while the former hop.

July 28th

A large moth flew into the house yesterday evening; it was completely black. I've never seen anything like it; possibly the Black Russet, *Aporophyla nigra.*

July 29th

Saw two Pipistrelle bats flying over the garden last night – first time I've ever seen more than one. That's progress, in the right direction.

July 31st

Poking about under a log, I find an intricate network of very fine white strands in the ground. This is fungal mycelium, and the individual strands are hyphae which merge thickly into the branching structure of the finest tree and shrub roots. It's a key element of the wildlife in this garden. Mycelium is the vegetative part of any fungus, while toadstools are the fruiting bodies which disperse reproductive spores. This network with associated beneficial bacteria effectively extends the root area of trees and other plants, taking sugars from them as a form of carbon which they cannot obtain for themselves, and in return supplying moisture and other nutrients which the mycelium glean from the soil; also carrying chemical information between the trees and conferring protection for them against disease. Nutrients supplied to the plants include phosphorous and nitrogen which the fungi have acquired from the soil by means of enzymes which trees do not possess. This means that the fungi have evolved this ability not for their own use but in order to make this offer to trees and plants. Without enhanced input of these two minerals, for instance, all trees in the world would be bonsai sized because they wouldn't have enough strength and wouldn't be able to grow enough to be the size they are.

Through this network trees can warn each other of large scale insect attack and recognise their relatives at other places in the network, which can be very extensive. Trees are able to communicate with one another, support their own distant offspring and even share food or moisture with species other than their own. So trees experience friendship of a kind; there's more co-operation than competition going on in a wood. It's social networking for trees. We could learn something from this.

The mycelium presence in the ground is vital as the chief agent of decomposition of plant material and the building of soil, holding it in place and preventing it washing away; it also provides a food source for many soil invertebrates. It's almost unbelievably profuse; one teaspoon of soil can contain ten kilometres of hyphae fibre if laid end to end. Each cell can regenerate a whole new network, so it's effectively immortal.

This symbiotic or mutually beneficial relationship between mycelium and plant roots is also known as the mycorrhizal network, or more nerdily as the Wood Wide Web. Mycorrhizal fungi make up between one half and one third of the mass of all living soil. 90% of all plants on Earth depend upon it; neither party would survive without the other. Some species of plant such as orchids have co-evolved their own unique mychorrhizae. it's 500 million years old – way older than the earliest dinosaurs – having evolved when life was beginning to adapt from the marine environment to living on land, so it effectively underpins most of today's land based life.

In non-wild settings including most cultivated gardens and agricultural settings this beneficial network can be completely obliterated by weedkillers, insecticides and fertilisers, all of which kill the fungi and associated bacteria, as well as by over-disturbance of the soil structure, all at huge cost to plant health and with far-reaching knock-on effects on other life forms, including ourselves.

Considered in this light, a vast forest can suddenly be conceived of as a single interactive superorganism rather than a group of separate individuals. With this relatively recent discovery, humankind is yet again being shown to have underestimated the complexity, the subtlety, the importance and the critical capabilities of key elements of our natural world. When are we going to learn that there's more we don't know than we do know, and that we're not the centre of the universe? And worse, that we're constantly in the process of destroying things we don't even begin to understand the importance of, or our dependence upon? We've got to change the supreme arrogance of believing that anything we can't yet prove the existence of doesn't exist, so we needn't worry about it.

It's also now recognised that natural mycorrhizal networks could play a vital role in countering the effect of climate change, and can be harnessed to undo its effects: such fungi already being cultivated on agricultural waste materials can create biodegradable alternatives to plastic packaging in as little as three days.

The role of fungi as a whole is hugely underestimated. They've been around for a billion years, which places them in the time when life on Earth was making the leap from single cell entities to multicellularity. Fungi and fungal spores are part of every human's personal ecosystem; they are all over our bodies and in our interior organs. Neanderthals are now known to have used fungal moulds that carried penicillin for their antibiotic properties. They were way ahead of us there.

The largest known living thing on earth is a fungus which covers ten square kilometres in Oregon. Fungi have amazing capabilities: they can make soil out of rock, manipulate animal behaviour including our own, push through tarmac and concrete. They can live a mile under the surface of the earth. Fungal cells have no brain, yet collectively they can make decisions and solve problems, such as finding the shortest distance between any two points in a labyrinth; they have a form of intelligence, though not as we narrowly think of it. They have other extraordinary properties which could be of great benefit to us in our ever-worsening predicament, such as neutralising pollution, heavy metals and other toxic substances, and breaking down plastics. Two hundred different types of fungus have been found growing on a single beetle. If we didn't have fungi to decompose vegetable matter, the planet would be covered with plant material up to the level of the human armpit in just three years. Knowing about fungi is a key element if we want to truly wish to understand the interconnectedness of all nature – and us. Check out Merlin Sheldrake's fascinating tome *Entangled Life*.

Eco-nerd, moi? Oui. The planet needs eco-nerds.

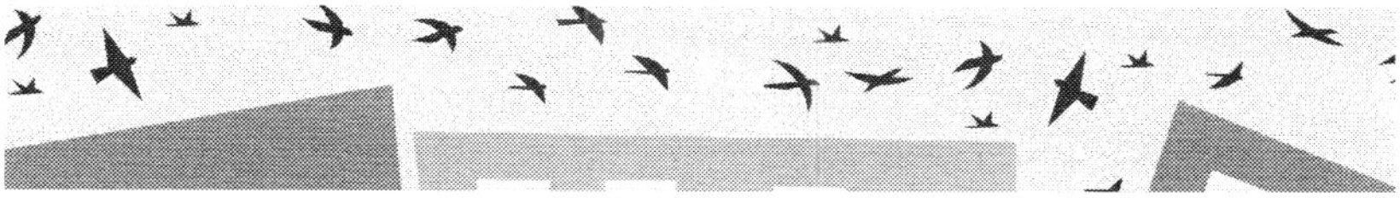

August

Aug 1st

The beginning of August is one of those pivotal stages in the natural year when the momentous plant growth and reproductive creature frenzy of spring and early summer have waned and bird nesting is over. Today, the ancient Celtic cross-quarter day of Lughnasadh marks this seasonal point, exactly midway between the summer solstice and the autumn equinox.

At 7am a small group of sparrows flies in to the top of the main tree where the main flock roosts every night throughout the whole year, which prompts them to hop up to the top twigs where they all gather to catch the early rays of the sun. I reckon the incomers are those who have nests on the go with late young still in them, so that they would have been roosting there. The whole assembly immediately starts their morning chatter update eg "How was your night? What did you dream about? Have you heard the weather report? What shall we do today? When any biggish bird flies over they all instantly drop back down into cover, to be on the safe side.

Aug 2nd

It's interesting to see once again how little the garden and the wildlife have been affected by the current heatwave. I've noticed over the years that this garden is extremely resilient to extremes of weather. The woodland-like surrounding hedge provides shelter from wind and shade from sun, and I've never seen any plant showing signs of heat stress in any of the considerable heat events we've had over the years. And we've never watered. Likewise, the deep rich leaf mould seems to be able to absorb endless soaking from the weeks of torrential downpour at other times of year, without any water lying. It's testimony to how valuable a part natural ecosystems can play in handling increasing different extremes of climate; this garden is not bothered by any of it. The mature nature garden - like the rest of nature when unspoiled - has a kind of self-adjusting stasis of near-perfection.

You can tell the birds and animals benefit from the protection the garden provides against months of high temperatures, and the presence of moisture. The birdbath is also popular with the sparrows using it daily, queuing up to take their turn drinking and splashing about to get rid of parasites, with blackbirds, starlings and other birds using it at other times. After washing, the sparrows find a sunny spot to fluff their feathers up and dry off. Wasps also come regularly to drink, but not bees; do they get their water in the nectar they feed on?

Aug 3rd

From the garden, in a rare moment when the sparrows are not in evidence, I hear high-pitched tinkling single-note calls coming from dense shrubbery in the quietest corner of the garden. This is from a pair of dunnocks, which I know frequent the garden though I hardly ever see them: another of those wonderful things that you're happy to just know is there. The dunnock or hedge sparrow is a brown bird which is often mistaken for the house sparrow - on the infrequent occasions when it's seen outside cover - but there are big differences: it's not a flocking bird and it completely lacks the sparrow's rowdy and boisterous behavioural patterns.

Aug 4th

The squirrel twins – the ones whose mother was trapped in spring by an unsympathetic gardener and transported to a galaxy far far away while the infants were still in their nest - have brought themselves up by supporting each other and foraging together. Now they're sitting together on the upstairs window-sill of my office, a couple of feet from me, grooming one another. They're so much less flighty than their mother was, and spend much more of their time in this garden than she did. It looks like they're learning fast and finding a lot to eat here, and they probably feel safe as the birds do. They're still adolescent size.

These youngsters are so endearing that I'm in danger of starting to like them.

Aug 5th

Happy plum-sucker news! The first fruits are ripening on this new plum tree and - surprise surprise - they're greengages, a delicious heritage plum variety that's not been grown commercially for many's the year. This means that our plum tree was grafted onto greengage stock and will crop much more heavily than its own offspring as the rootstock is always more vigorous than the grafted on *scion,* the small shoot taken from an existing tree of the required variety. Suckers grow from below the grafting point and most people get rid of them - what a waste.

Aug 6th

In the garden the butterflies don't seem to be minding the heatwave; I guess they're solar powered for a start – very sustainable. Among the butterflies I'm seeing at present, the Holly Blues aka Ivy Blues are my favourite – those small blue creatures seen earlier in the summer, which lay eggs and hatch twice a year, laying on holly earlier in the season and now a later flush laying on the ivy. They're really the same species, named according to when they're seen. A delightful pair of them is flying together in the air, clearly with mating intent. I guess it helps to have a profusion of both these plant species in the garden.

At a distance they look pure blue, but if you see them up close – difficult, as they're frenetic flyers who never keep still for long, always behaving as if there's an awful lot to be done and a very short time to do it in – they have tiny pale ivory dots. Very pretty.

Aug 8th

My summer reading is A *Sand County Almanac* by Aldo Leopold, one of the world's great pioneering conservationists, a joy to read and poignantly relevant to today. It's a beautifully written and intimate portrayal of the wildlife around the author in 1945, a timeless classic. It's extraordinary to read what he said about humankind and species extinction in those days before I was born. Leopold writes:

"It is a century now since Darwin gave us the first glimpse of the origin of species. We know now what was unknown to all the preceding caravan of generations: that men are only fellow-voyagers with other creatures in the odyssey of evolution. This new knowledge should have given us, by this time, a sense of kinship with fellow-creatures; a wish to live and let live; a sense of wonder over the magnitude and duration of the biotic enterprise."

Modern science is finally beginning to acknowledge what ancient sciences recognised thousands of years ago: that the total interconnectedness of ourselves and the natural world is not a metaphor; it's real and it's physical. Quantum physics tells us that our physical being does not, as we generally think, end at the edge of our solid bodies; our bodies are not solid, but a spacious collection of sub-atomic particles which are perpetually interacting with all the other particles in this universe. And perhaps other universes too:

"What we call objects are in fact points of correlation in an unbroken and interconnected network of events, motions, relations and energies – the continuum of nature. Subatomic particles and all matter made from them, including our cells, tissues and bodies, are patterns of activity rather than things. There is no thing that exists by itself. Living nature and the universe as a whole form a seamless dynamic web of interrelated parts and rhythmic processes" – James Oschman.

Sorry, Aldo; it looks like we still haven't got that kinship going on any kind of global scale just yet. But some of us are working on it.

Aug 10th

Today in the garden I'm walking amongst lots of different butterflies, which is pure joy, including a pair of Large White butterflies, one larger and whiter than the other, engaged in a delightful mating dance flight.

I'm also delighted to see the Speckled Wood butterfly (*Pararge Aegeria*) in the centre of the garden which simulates those open glades in wild woodland that are so important for this and other butterflies and flying insects. The brown butterflies can be difficult to tell apart; this particular species has three small white-ringed 'eyespots' on each hindwing and one on each forewing. They like patches of sunlight on woodland edges – just what we've provided.

Aug 11th

With this year's young, the sparrows' flock size looks to have doubled over last year's tribe. Maybe my magpie dissuasion campaign during this year's spring breeding season - and the attacks on them by the carrion crows of course - played a part in reducing the usual fledgling decimation. However the increased flock size, with the enhanced proportion of naive juveniles, will inevitably attract the attentions of the local sparrow-hawk. But the population will undoubtedly be able to cope with this. Life goes on.

Aug 13th

As the heatwave continues in the world outside, a cool micro-climate pervades the garden interior. Today the hen blackbird is gorging herself on a few pecked apples that have now gone bad and are fermenting on the branches. It seems to me she's after alcohol content, but this bird is certainly fussy about which decaying apple to settle on, trying them all. I can't see any difference between them – they all look equally rotten to me, but she's extremely discerning, like: "I'm looking for certified Dorset Rough Scrumpy Grade content, and nothing less will do!" She finally settles on one, starts eating into it, then consumes the whole thing. Evidently it's extremely more-ish, as alcohol often is. Doesn't seem to cause mother's ruin, though.

Aug 14th

In the garden, our silver birch log - imbued with shiitake spores two years ago - has born fruit at last: three mature shiitake mushrooms. Before removing them I notice what looks like fine smoke rising from them, caught in a patch of slanting early morning sunlight. Then I realise it isn't smoke; it's billions upon billions of shiitake spores. And they just kept pouring out. It's another manifestation of nature's amazingness that is so inspiring.

I love blackbirds' foraging style. They look at the ground, poke around, then make a little rush to the next likely looking spot as if there's not a moment to be lost. If they don't find anything there they make another little rush, then maybe find a worm there and eat it, and then make another rush to the next spot - even if it's only two feet away.

It's almost as if they're genetically programmed to spend as high a percentage of their time as possible at these spots and as low a percentage as possible getting between them. Like all wild creatures, they're driven by life-and-death equations of time and energy usage v energy gains.

Aug 15th

It's easy to live in each moment in the garden: hearing the blackbird singing his dawn chorus outside the bedroom window even when you're still in the borderlands of sleep, enjoying the fleeting visits of butterflies in the midday sunshine, watching the sparrows settle down in their roosts as dusk approaches. These creatures live pretty much entirely in the present moment too; they aren't thinking about what's happening next week or next month; for them it's all about the here and now.

Today the small birds are particularly twitchy, looking non-stop all around. I think they're worried there's a hawk about.

I'm reminded that I met a sparrow-hawk face to face in the garden last year. I was walking along the side of the house, just rounding a corner of the building, when a female came shooting round the corner from the opposite direction at exactly my head height. She instantly flicked past me and flew on, passing within a foot of my face, demonstrating its amazing agility and speed of reaction.

I had a virtually identical and even more memorable experience very many years ago with a scaled-up predator, the peregrine falcon. I was arriving at the rocky end of a wild coastal headland in the west of Ireland as dusk was beginning to fall, when a flash of blue-grey body and dark stripes on a pale chest came barrelling round from the opposite direction, likewise dodging my head with lightning reflex. I didn't see what either of these birds was chasing.

These raw vivid wildlife experiences touch something ancient within; they get seared into your visual memory and are never forgotten. Likewise I still recall the childhood experience of my father bringing home a sadly dead but perfect barn owl which he found by the roadside at night. With its incredibly detailed white and gold feathers, it seemed like the most beautiful thing I had ever seen.

Some years later as a teenager I was walking through the Mourne Mountains in Northern Ireland at the end of a beautiful day with the sun setting. The path went on a long way ahead of me, straight as an arrow's course, cut sharp and clear through impenetrable shoulder high bracken by users of the path. I looked far ahead and saw that a badger was ambling along the pathway towards me, head down, hundreds of yards away. I stopped and watched; the badger came closer and closer; finally, it walked right up to me, still with its head down; it stopped, raised its head, sniffed and detected my presence, looked like this was not what it was expecting, turned round and ran all the way back along the path. Again, maybe twenty years ago, I was walking on the Isle of Mull. I climbed the side of a steep ridge and stepped over the peak; where I was about to put my foot down, a golden eagle rose up from under me and flew away, even more surprised to see me than I was to see her. And in more recent times as I lay on my back in the long grass of a meadow in Norfolk, I felt the air move as the ghostly shape of a barn owl floated in silence over my face, inches away, as it hunted for prey. These images, burned onto the retina of the mind, are priceless. And the great thing is that at any moment on any day, even if not much is presently going on, there is a possibility of another of them happening. That's the joy of wildlife encounters.

Aug 17th

I hear via neighbourhood WhatsApp that the sparrow-hawk is indeed in the vicinity; he's currently right in the garden next door. At present he's just sitting on their fence, perfectly aware that he's being watched, so he can't be looking for prey, because when he's doing that no-one will see him till the last second. These hawks have an incredibly fierce look, it seems to us, with their piercing yellow or orange eyes. But it's not fierce; it's just their normal look, the look of repose. It's just calmly going about following its job description - killing things - and the eyes are practically designed to optimise that process. At this point in time he's not looking for something to kill; it's much more likely that he's recovering breath after making an unsuccessful attack, which takes a lot out of these birds. We've all been there, haven't we?

Aug 18th

People wonder why birds can seem to completely disappear from their gardens and parks at this time of year. Well, the answer is moulting. Most of our regular birds here are not nearly as evident as they were even a week or two ago, yet food is still disappearing from the seed feeder. Feathers don't last for ever; by the end of the breeding season birds' resources become severely depleted; the feathers get worn out or weakened by all the extra activity and by the privations of feather mites which proliferate in nests and close contact with young, which means they can't fly so well to hunt or escape predation. Late summer is prime time for moulting the old feathers and re-growing new ones. This is a highly energy-draining process and is best done when it's relatively warm and dry, and when there are still plenty of protein-rich insects about to fuel the new feather growth.

Moulting makes it harder for birds to fly, so they know they're more vulnerable to predators and more subject to the effects of inclement weather. That's why they tend to remain hidden in the vegetation much more than usual, and more cautious about being seen or coming out to feed. The feathers are replaced one by one rather than all at once; this can take six to eight weeks. After that they'll be ready to face the cooler weather and the other challenges of autumn and winter - and will have better quality plumage for next year's breeding displays.

Aug 20th

Colours in the garden are becoming less washed out now as August draws on and cools down, producing the vivid red berries on the rowan tree, the life-enhancing green of the foliage in the garden, the exotic tints sported by the goldfinches.

The dawn chorus has now completely gone, except for the usual cheerful daily chatter from the sparrows – much later than dawn as always - and the gulls, which always seem to find a reason to start up their raucous squawking well ahead of dawn. These calls sound angry and belligerent to us, but is it possible they're just expressing the pure joy of being alive? A long shot, I admit, but possible. Maybe if I look at it this way I can stop being so annoyed at them and get back to sleep more easily.

August 22nd

When squirrels first started raiding the seed feeders a few years ago I came up with a simple technique for preventing it, and I don't know why more people don't use it. I simply suspended the seed feeder from a branch on a long enough string for the squirrels not to be able to reach down to it. And it worked – up to now. But the creative young squirrel twins have found a way of stretching themselves out from an adjacent branch on their back legs, with their forelegs on the feeder, like a living bridge. Then they can stick their faces into the feeding cavity.

I sympathise with these young squirrels, but don't want the feeders completely emptied by them. So I installed a longer string so they can't reach it any more. But they can still feed underneath it, where they get plenty of sunflower seeds in their hulls which get knocked out by the sparrows in their search for smaller seeds. An ethical solution.

Aug 25th

The weather has dramatically changed; the time of storms has begun early. Climate change and extreme weather patterns are showing up in the frequency, severity and extended duration of the storm season. In decades past in autumn we used to get one or two that would blow over in a day; now there are many more and they wreak all kinds of havoc and flooding all over the British Isles.

The current storm brought strong dry winds here, producing severe windburn on the foliage of trees, shrubs and smaller garden plants all over town. However our stout jungle once more provided protection not only to the trees and shrubs but to the creatures that call them their home. Haven't seen any windburn at all.

The sparrows are splashing together in the birdbath in the bright sun that quickly ensues as soon as the storm has passed over.

Aug 27th

Today, an encounter with a huge caterpillar of the Privet Hawk Moth (*Sphinx ligustri*) which has a 12 centimetre wingspan - the size of your hand - which can make a hissing sound when disturbed. This caterpillar is nearly

10 cm in length, vivid green in colour and with white and purple diagonal go-faster stripes and a white horn at one end: a magnificent creature. It had fallen out of a lilac bush (an alternative food plant for this species) so I put it back there.

Later in the day, researching the species, I realise that I might have done a Slightly Bad Thing: in August the larvae drop to the earth where they bury themselves, preparing for their pupa stage. Oh well, by now it's probably just dropped out of the bush again - possibly after swearing at me for putting it back up there.

Aug 29th

Wishing to see wildlife further afield once more, we revisit the rewilded Knepp estate. The biggest excitement is that White Storks are nesting there and are raising young in the UK for the first time in nearly 600 years. Knepp will also be introducing beavers this autumn.

Rewilding is becoming a big thing in UK, as in many other countries. Beavers have just been granted "permanent right to remain" in the Devon river they've been in as infiltrators for five years. A major grant has been given to introduce European bison in Kent. White-tailed Sea Eagles have been introduced on the Isle of Wight, and there are hopes for lynx in the Scottish highlands.

But our garden wildlife reserve is great too – I love the blackbird tucking into an apple, the sparrows with their current crop of youngsters, the hedgehog visiting in earlier summer, and much else – as much as I love anything else in my life, and they bring just as much joy.

Aug 30th

Ate first blackberries of the year from the garden today. I encourage brambles growing in the lower hedges of the garden because they're great for protecting nest sites of small birds like wren and robin. The berries are particularly numerous this year.

Aug 31st

In the local paper today on the letters page I read, gobsmacked:

"We went for a paddle in the sea today, and there wasn't a single shrimp to be seen. What are things coming to? We used to catch thousands and thousands of them in our shrimping nets, and now there aren't any." ... written without a hint of irony. Some people just don't get it: their individual actions do make a difference – for worse or for better. To them it's all about 'why don't somebody do something about this?' ...whoever 'somebody' is.

Pédantesque, moi? Non, didactique.

September

Sept 1st

Found a broken woodpigeon egg shell on the ground – white, about 4cm long – a sign that the pair based in this garden are still attempting breeding. I reckon this latest attempt has been unsuccessful due to either the nest falling apart or predation by magpies. Woodpigeons mainly breed from April to October, but have been recorded breeding in these islands in every single month of the year.

The feral town pigeons, nesting under the railway bridge nearby, do even better; their shelter is so cosy through winter - and their food sources so diverse and plentiful - that they can keep breeding all year round, every year. They're a very successful subspecies, as is evident in every town and city in the land. They're not much admired, though; is this because as humans we only value that which is scarce, in decline? Or worse, only it's when in danger of extinction and usually too late to make a difference? Yes, that does sound like us.

Sept 3rd

Weather continues to be bright but showery. As usual, when any morning sun first reaches into the garden the whole flock of sparrows hop upwards from their roosting spots low in the interior of the hawthorn tree onto the tips that project beyond the dense canopy, to catch those early rays.

I love the way sparrows will just stay sitting together like this for ages; they will remain there until something eventually happens to get them to move. Usually some of the flock will suddenly fly off, and you can see the remaining birds look at each other and become twitchy, as if wondering whether they should fly off too, in case they might miss something. The remainers look round them; some lean forward as if about to take off, then change their minds and stay. Usually the ones that left come back and join the flock, and you can see the ones that didn't leave settling down and thinking: yes, we did the right thing there, what a relief. It's all part of the dilemma of being a flocking bird. We've all been there. But it shows that sparrows have evolved a highly successful model for living in that they can take all this time out before really needing to go and get breakfast.

To flock or not to flock, that is the question. It's one of the fundamental evolutionary choices for all birds, and affects almost everything in their lives. For instance, if you watch a solitary blackbird feeding on the ground on plentiful food, it will lift its head and look up between every single downward peck of its beak, to watch out for predators. But if you see a flock of starlings feeding together over the ground, they nearly all keep their heads down for nearly all the time, because somebody is always keeping an eye out for danger; they simply have more eyes to do that with. The sparrows are the same. This means they can feed more continuously, and therefore spend a higher percentage of their time feeding: a crucial parameter for species success. And sure enough, I've noticed that when the blackbird is feeding among sparrows or starlings it hardly looks up between pecks at the ground.

Making the choice of whether to develop an individual or a flocking lifestyle involves many other factors, but within similar species groups different sub-choices will be made. For instance blackbirds and redwings are both members of the thrush family, but the latter become flocks during the winter to migrate together to where food is more plentiful, while blackbirds go solo apart from the mating season. On open land, many small bird species such as tits or finches will join with other diverse species to make temporary flocks for safety and more efficient food finding in winter.

But birds such as starlings, sparrows and rooks are entirely flocking species and this generally brings them success. Yet blackbirds are a highly successful species here in Europe. This may be partly explained by the way they've adapted to life in private gardens: a habitat which is increasingly beneficial in contrast to industrialised monoculture farmland which is providing almost nothing for birds and other wildlife.

Sept 5th

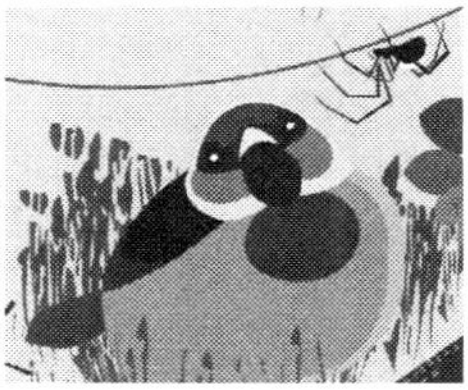

The sparrow breeding season this year has been so successful that a splinter group has just moved into the garden of the next-door-neighbour-but-one. This neighbour has recently allowed dense shrubbery to grow, which will make a good home for them, and she puts out seed feeders. It's great to see the wildlife expanding beyond our garden to populate the surrounding ecosystem.

Sept 7th

Today I encounter the council's workmen spraying along the edges of the pavements on our street with glyphosate: a most unwelcome measure for anyone valuing life. I make sure to talk to the operatives even though I know they're not the ones who make the decision; you have to speak up or they will assume everyone is happy with these measures.

They specially focus on the back edge of the pavement, right up against everyone's fence line: the only part of the paving which has vegetation and can therefore offer a home to roadside invertebrates, and also the route which hedgehogs take at night moving from one garden territory to another, foraging and trying not to be too obvious. As if their lives weren't hard enough already.

This damaging practice exemplifies once more the widely held belief that we must sanitise our external environment, that everything around us must be neat and tidy and sterile. If the council doesn't do this stuff they'll be greeted by outraged representations from the apoplectic section of the citizenry. This is exactly the same distorted moralistic attitude that first led humanity to embark on global scale trashing: seeing nature and wildness as something nasty and ungodly, to be subdued and suppressed. It's probably connected with an ancient association of wildness with fear, which does not have to be the case; it's perfectly possible to be comfortable and at ease in the wild.

Sept 9th

At 7.30am, caught in dappled early morning sunlight under the apple tree, a cloud of tiny insects dances in mating flights. I'm guessing that they're of the broad category officially known as *non-biting gnats*. It's glorious to watch.

It's heartening to see such autumn profusion manifesting in these little beasties. In South America there are orchids that are pollinated only by such tiny gnats, and so have evolved correspondingly miniscule flower parts. But guess what, there are people who even regard non-biting gnats as a pest and go to a lot of trouble to eradicate them through sprayed insecticides with corresponding collateral damage to other species from invertebrates, up the food chain.

Sept 11th

First day of ivy blossom opening, in the mostly warm and sunny weather we're having at present. Ivy starts providing for wildlife by flowering in the season when most other plant sources are going to seed and closing down. Nectar from the flowers is being enjoyed today by multitudes of honeybees, bumblebees and hoverflies. It's as if they've been watching the ivy, waiting in the wings for this moment and then all descending on it at once. I wonder if you can buy honey that's just made from bees at the time they're feeding on ivy nectar? I'm sure it would have an extraordinary flavour, because it has a delicious scent and insects are going wild for it today.

The flowers are followed of course by berries in midwinter, and the dense foliage is regularly used by overwintering invertebrates including butterflies such as Peacock, Red Admiral and Small Tortoiseshell – plus the Ivy Bee, a relatively new arrival to these islands, and something of a conundrum: a solitary bee seen together in large numbers, around the ivy, and a more positive effect of the northward effect of climate change. So ivy is the great provider at times of the year when almost everything else isn't.

Sept 12th

On the house roof a late-born adolescent black-backed gull, not yet flying properly, follows a woodpigeon along the ridge line, calling incessantly to be fed in that supremely unlovely and pitiful way only young gulls have. I marvel at how parents of these creatures can sit beside them and completely ignore for this attention-seeking noise. They must have some way of switching off and being unaffected. Transcendental meditation, perhaps?

Sept 14th

Another sunny morning. At 8.30am sparrows are systematically hunting for spiders all round the gutters on the conservatory. That's an early start for them. The spiders will be going indoors soon; maybe they're starting to move already, and therefore more visible to the eagle-eyed sparrows.

Sept 16th

A frog is doing a good job on slug control in the undergrowth. Mind you, the hedgehog, blackbirds and others also help with that. Froglets here must disperse widely because we hardly see them in the garden until it's spawning time the following year.

Sept 18th

There's wonderful appeal from - and many insights to be gained into - the lives of the mundane and everyday species that frequent our garden, like sparrows and hoverflies. But once in a while something special and unexpected pops in to this little urban habitat of ours.

Today that something special was an Emperor Dragonfly, *Anex Imperatur,* Britain's bulkiest and most stunningly beautiful dragonfly. This marvel spent time coasting round the garden in the morning sunlight, catching flying insects in the air around the flowering ivy and pausing to rest there between hunting flights. The magnificent creature is coloured apple green and sky blue with black markings, and is up to 70 millimetres in length and wing span. The sighting is particularly unusual as we're far from any of its usual larger scale watery habitats, and it's the wrong time of year for laying eggs in our new little pond. Maybe it's drawn here by the richness of flying prey, which it not only catches but also eats on the wing. Truly wonderful. Now, back to the glorious mundane.

Sept 21st

Autumn equinox, another major turning point of the year: the astronomical end of summer and beginning of fall, when the sun crosses the celestial equator and day and night are of equal duration.

Today I spot an item prompting biodiversity excitement: a small yew tree seedling. This shows just how important birds and their excretory processes are for spreading trees and shrubs. There are no yew trees anywhere near our home, so the yew berry that carried this seed must have been eaten elsewhere, probably by a member of the thrush family. Many people know that every part of the yew tree is poisonous to humans, but few know that this excludes the beautiful and succulent red berry or aril – provided you don't consume the seed as well. I've not taken this risk and I'm not recommending that you do.

I'm not holding my breath with this seedling as yew trees are not considered fully mature until they're 900 years old.

Sept 23rd

Amazingly, Drooping Wing Blackbird is still around. Most authorities believe that these birds typically move territories much more than this one has. Maybe this domain is just too good to leave. Today he's vigorously attacking a fermenting apple that promises inebriation and perhaps intestinal gas. The time of decay is upon us; referencing Keats's famous poem you could call it the season of mists and mellow flatulence.

Sept 24th

The ivy flowers are super-abundant now. After a rain-shower, masses of insects are continuing to visit them, ranging from tiny fruit-flies and midges to honey-bees and diverse bumblebees. The collective buzzing is tremendous, a delight to immerse oneself in.

Sept 25th

Still looking for fresh live protein, the sparrows are feasting on late aphids on the apple leaves. Must be the result of the Indian Summer weather we're getting at the moment, one of the joys of European weather systems - some years.

These tiny invertebrates represent more than their share of the autumnal profusion. A single female aphid can produce 600 billion offspring in a season. Have you ever wondered how they can reproduce so quickly? The even more surprising fact is that they're mostly celibate and reproduce sexlessly by cloning: cutting out the middle man, or indeed any man. Aphids are considered a horror by most conventional gardeners (mainly because they've managed to kill all the aphid predator invertebrates with pesticides) but very welcome in a wild garden where they're an important food source for other insects and for birds, which is why they don't get out of control in these settings. Dave Goulson cites evidence that confirms this (see bibliography). Pesticidal gardeners would do well to wake up, smell the coffee, join the dots and get the finger out. In natural gardens super-numerous aphids are part of a win-win solution for them, for the many bird and insect species that feed on them, and for the wild gardener who watches it all.

Sept 26th

At 7.45am a wren is hopping round the elder tree just outside my bedroom window: always a cause of joy. I often suspect that these birds are in the garden somewhere, but most of the time don't see them. Not being seen is number one criterion on the wren's troglo-

dytic job description; it flits so quickly under cover from twig to twig, hardly ever out in the open. This further suggests that our practice of densifying the lower hedges with cuttings from the pruned tops every year is doing what we hoped it would.

Many other wild creatures are also good at not being seen, some obsessively so. This is exemplified in the book I'm currently reading: *The Snow Leopard* by Peter Matthieson, a wildlife classic about his field trip into the Himalaya mountains and the Tibetan plateau. For the author the almost mystical elusiveness of the titular animal is more appreciated than a sighting (which never happens) would be. It's also about how important nature and wildlife can be to mental, emotional and spiritual well-being. I definitely agree with that; having access to our wild garden helps with me deal with life's varied challenges, which seem all the more numerous in this day and age.

Not seeing some species yet knowing they're there can bring an important form of satisfaction in itself. Yet our modern visual-biased society is obsessed with actually seeing things: "Did you go to ABC?" these people ask. "Yes." you reply. "- Did you see the ZYZs?" "- No." "- Oh dear, what a shame." No, not necessarily. Or, worse still: "Did you go to PQR?" "- Yes." "- Did you see the STUs?" "- Yes." "- Did you get a photo? " "- No.""-Well that was a waste of time then, wasn't it?" No, it wasn't. Fuck off.

I'm happy to know that the wrens and the hedgehogs and the Lesser Spotted Knotted Wotsits are there somewhere in the neighbourhood, even though we may not often see them. And in the case of many rarer species it's a relief to just know that they still exist at all, somewhere on the planet.

Sept 27th

Clash of the predators: as I watch from indoors the sparrow-hawk is chased by magpies into the ash tree which stands on the road outside our garden. I walk into the garden and the magpies, ever skittish, immediately fly off; but the sparrow-hawk surprises me by staying as I walk under the tree to have a look at it. Maybe there was prey it was reluctant to abandon, having invested the energy in killing it: 90% of attacks by sparrow-hawks are unsuccessful. Also interesting to see the conflict between these too, suggesting that the sparrows may be getting a degree of protection from their chief nemesis (the sparrow-hawk) via their number two nemesis (the magpies) on this occasion.

Sept 28th

The squirrel twins, still not fully grown, continue to act together as a foraging unit. As I watch, one is picking up sunflower seeds from under the bird feeder even as the other is grooming it and removing parasites. It's so endearing that I'm in increasing danger of liking them. It's difficult to tell their respective genders at any distance, but I suspect there's one of each as one is noticeably larger than the other.

I find myself wondering whether they will be able to survive their first winter. But later in the day I see that they're constructing a drey for that season, pulling green leaves and twigs from different shrubs into the dense ivy-covered branching-out point of the apple tree. Having supplementary rations from the bird feeder fall-out and apples that stay on the tree into early spring will help. I'm now seeing them hiding away stuff that will keep, like sunflower seeds in their shells.

Squirrels can check nuts and seeds without having to open them first, to see if they're free of decay or parasitic insects and therefore worth storing. If they're damaged they will eat the good parts on the spot, but if there's nothing worthwhile inside the shell the nut will be abandoned. This is why you often see intact hazelnuts on the ground below the tree, but if you open them there's nothing inside.

Squirrels eating seeds now while burying others for later makes tree reproduction more successful in the environment as a whole despite so many being consumed and therefore not germinating. In our garden we get a large number of healthy hazel saplings every year from the process. One squirrel can bury up to 3,000 nuts each year, and it's only going to find a fraction of these. It buries them at optimum germination depth too. Isn't nature wonderful?

Sept 29th

Today the squirrel twins appear to be having rough sex on my upstairs office windowsill. On closer inspection, however, they're only play-acting: practising for when Mr or Ms Right-Squirrel comes along?

Michaelmas, or the feast of St Michael, is an example of early European Christianity accessing the pre-established power of Pagan dates and channelling it into Christian festival days and quarter-year markers. In this case it has been chosen because it's near the equinox, but the best known example is that of Christmas which harnessed the pre-Christian traditions of the winter solstice even though Jesus is known to have been born in May.

From the Middle Ages to the early twentieth century it was always reckoned that harvests had to be completed by Michaelmas. As it's the time when darker and colder nights begin, Saint Michael was rolled out to replace earlier spiritual entities as the protector against darkness and negative forces. He's also the patron saint of grocers: work that one out.

This year the fruitfulness of autumn is especially striking; there is a superabundance of apples, blackberries, damsons, haw and holly berries, hazelnuts and every kind of wild fruit or nut. I've had my suspicions, and now I'm sure: this is turning out to be what is known as a *mast year* for our part of the country.

A mast year is when all the different fruit- or nut-bearing trees mysteriously synchronise production of an exceptionally heavy crop. Mast years happen in their respective areas at intervals of around four to seven years. This means that at these intervals there will be one year when the exceptional numbers of synchronised fruits, nuts and seeds create a high chance that enough will be left over from being eaten for germinations to ensure reproductive success - for all these species at once. The name 'mast' derives from the Old English word *maest* referring to the fruit of trees like oak and beech, which in medieval times were of great importance to commoners who had the right to take their pigs out on the wooded commons for fattening in the autumn.

This is an extraordinarily sophisticated evolutionary development for the trees to have made; producing large quantity of seed represents a big drain on resources so there's great advantage not doing this to extreme every year, especially in years when the conditions do not favour seed production and survival is a higher priority. But the most amazing thing is that so many different species of tree and shrub – in the UK not only beech and oak, but all the others too, such as sweet and horse chestnut, rowan, hawthorn, blackthorn, hazel, crab-apple, wild cherry, elder and more – all manage to take this step in the same year. Trees and shrubs many miles apart join in the same rhythm of normal seeding or super-seeding; the fruiting in a mast year means that there will be no overall growth in that year. In south-east Asia, entire forests with hundreds of different tree species mast together over irregular periods that range from two to twelve years.

So what determines which years the trees in any area will collectively choose as a mast year? Scientists say that it isn't known how this works, but then scientists are often the last to collectively acknowledge stuff. What they do know is that it's partly about the conditions which are most favourable for that extra productive effort: probably a combination of a warm spring for copious flowering with no subsequent cold snap that would damage the flowers or nascent fruits, followed by optimal combinations of summer and autumnal sunshine and rain for filling out and ripening.

But there must be more to it than this, because it's surely extraordinary that all these different species unanimously concur on when to go for it and when not to go for it, as individual species would have somewhat varying preferences. It's almost as if they had a means of sharing info. Well, in fact, not almost; they do have such a means. We now know that trees do indeed communicate with one another – and share resources – through the vast underground network of thread-like fungi known as *mycelia*, which I've described earlier. I'd say this plays the major part in how unanimous plant agreement is reached on which are to be the mast years.

A mast year has a big knock-on effect on local animals and birds. There will be much more immediate food than in a regular year, and there will be more to store away for squirrels, jays and the like. There will be relatively quick effects on mouse populations as they have such a short breeding cycle, and therefore on predators such as owls and kestrels who rely on these, so those will do well too. But these mammal populations usually crash in the following year when the trees and shrubs return to normal production, and this in turn affects the predator numbers. So in a subtle way this too works to the long-term benefit of the seed producing plants, disrupting the population patterns of the creatures eating their precious output so they don't become too numerous.

Sept 30th

I'm seeing tiny wasps visiting the solitary bumblebee holes in the ground to lay their very unwelcome eggs with these hosts. Parasitism is an amazingly popular lifestyle choice in nature; indeed it's now thought that about half of all species are parasitic, making parasitism the most fashionable of all ways of getting something to eat. Parasites are also the most species rich group of organisms because they're constantly evolving subspecies and variants in order to become more specialised and carve out an ever more distinct niche for themselves. Talk about biting the hand that feeds you!

Cuckoos are perhaps our best-known parasitic birds. Vast numbers of bacteria and viruses are parasites. Very many plants tap into the roots, stems, trunks, branches, or leaves of other plants, such as the much loved (but not by the host tree) mistletoe. All plant-eating insects are technically parasites; there are currently thought to be up to 30 million different species of these. Some ants parasitise other ant colonies, using them as cheap labour; actually, free labour. Some parasites use a host mosquito as a kind of mobile hypodermic syringe to reach their real host; that's how we get malaria, for instance. A whole host of parasites live first on one animal only because they want to get inside another animal that kills and eats that first host animal. And don't get me started on sexual parasitism..

Some parasites kill their host and others don't; maybe in some cases, somewhere back along the line of evolutionary development of particular species, the choice depended on how they were feeling on a particular day: like, 'Make my day, punk!' When parasites kill their host it's known as *parasitoidism*, which sounds like it's they're more paranoid than other parasites. Paranoia might be appropriate in some cases, leading to the not-very-famous last words: 'Eek! What am I going to eat now I've killed my host?'

Parasitoid species are extraordinarily numerous but exceptionally little-known; what we do know for certain is that most of those in existence have yet to be discovered, yet alone named. The whole phenomenon is amazing, and as usual we don't know enough yet to fully understand just how amazing it really is – yet in the meantime we're destroying it.

One of the most surprisingly creative aspects of parasitism is how many parasites parasitise other parasites, like the protozoa living in the digestive tract of the flea which in turn lives on a dog. The majority of parasitoids are wasps of one kind or another. Being a parasitic wasp in itself offers a huge range of lifestyle choices; a researcher has found an oak gall which contained oak gall wasps which had been parasitised by other smaller wasps, which had been parasitised by even smaller wasps, which had been parasitised by tinier wasps still, which had been parasitised by unbelievably small wasps, which were probably trying to win the *Most Specialised Niche in All of Nature* award, and may have succeeded, at least until they too got parasitised upon. I can't get enough of this stuff.

Sur le spectrum, moi? Peut-etre.

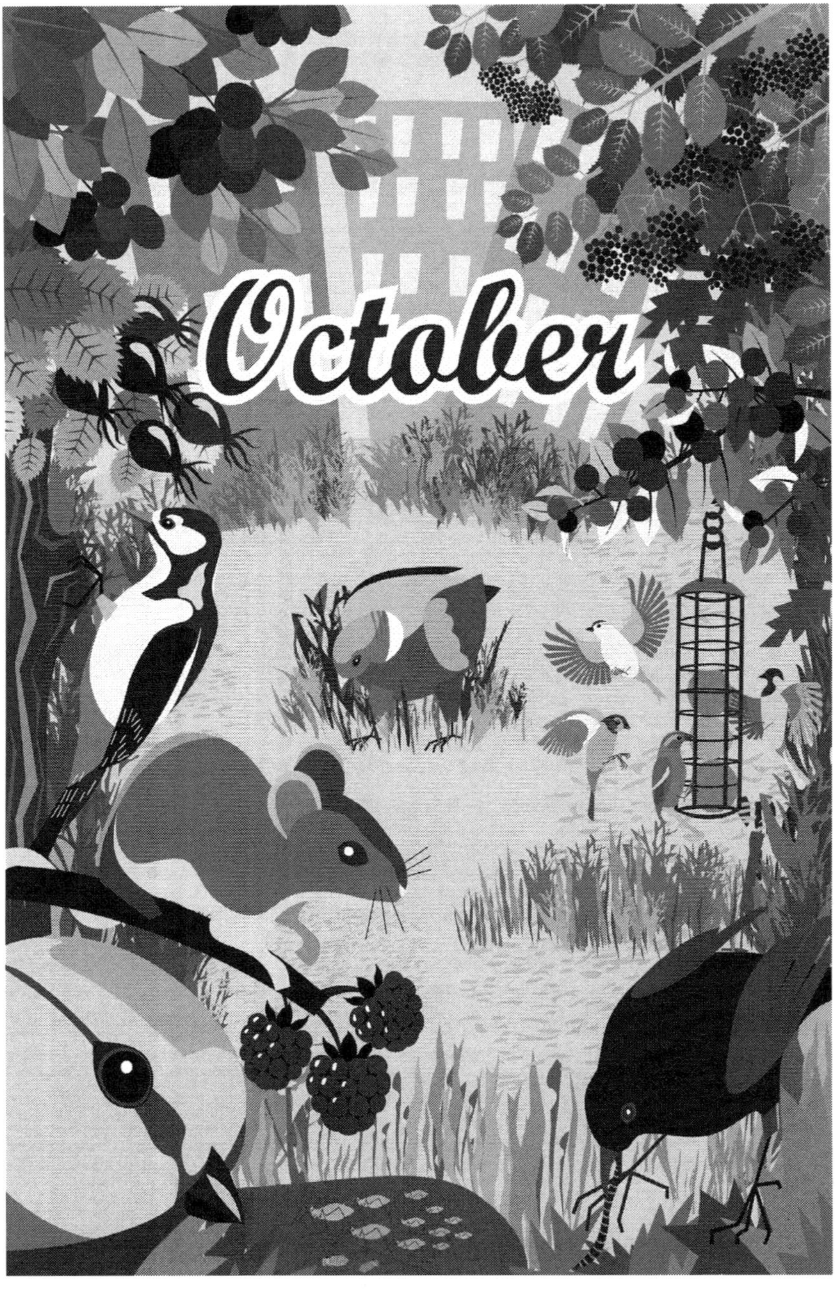
October

Oct 1st

A warm sunny interlude after a couple of wet days brings great numbers of worker honey-bees and hoverflies swarming over the ivy blossom - especially profuse in this mast year - drawn by its scent which is now peaking. Word will have got around the hive by way of waggle-dance, bringing the bees out in numbers for this treasure. Ivy is the single main autumnal source of pollen and nectar for flower-visiting insects in these islands. The flowers only occur on the mature ivy branches, characterised by having oval leaves, as opposed to the immature branches and younger plants which display the more familiar five-pointed leaf formation.

I'm wondering where these honey-bees have come from, and whether they're wild or not – and how you can tell the difference. In fact you can't, unless you're able to follow the bees back to their hive, which is difficult to say the least. In practice, though, few bees these days are from wild hives, especially in urban areas. In fact when a wild colony is reported it will hopefully be captured by local bee-keepers, placed in a man-made hive and put to work, albeit with free health services such as protection against varroa parasites and sugar to get the bees through the winter.

Oct 2nd

All the birds are less shy now, having completed their late summer moult and regrowth of all new feathers. Two cock blackbirds - one of them our dear old friend Drooping Wing Blackbird - are having a singing competition, DWB in this garden and the other bird quite a few gardens away. DWB sings a phrase, then waits while the rival endeavours to repeat it, which it does precisely. DWB then utters a longer and more complex phrase, and the listening bird repeats that one too, though sounding a little more emphatic as if to say, 'I can do what you can do but I can do it better because I have more blackbird testosterone than you'. This continues with ever longer and more complicated song passages, all faithfully reproduced by the rival bird. To me the songs continue to sound achingly beautiful even though I know that in reality they're full of venom and vitriol, and blackbird swearing.

Oct 3rd

DWB'S rival from yesterday is still imitating his song and coming closer and closer to his nemesis, till he's in our garden and clearly getting on DWB's nerves, as in "Stop repeating everything I say, I'm trying to cement a relationship here!". I'm standing in the garden at the foot of the elder tree, watching both higher up in its branches. Suddenly the birds are tangled in fierce combat – and blackbird fights can be to the death - then tumbling together down through the branches of the tree I'm under. They land at my feet still locked in battle, so engrossed they don't see me.

Nearby, the hen bird appears uninterested in the contest and carries on feeding as usual; she will presumably take up with whichever wins the fight, but doesn't seem to have any vested interest. It's a bit like a gladiatorial event where the audience has a short attention span – and also similar to the way very young children can watch others getting hurt with complete lack of empathy. The two are still spatting when I go back inside the house. You don't often see a blackbird fight this serious, especially outside breeding season.

DWB has held on to this prized territory for a surprisingly long time, considering that we're told that the blackbirds we see in our gardens are changing all the time. So this very recognisable individual has provided evidence of a long reign here. But will today prove to bring his downfall at last?

Oct 4th

DWB prevailed and the interloper sloped off. Hooray, I think, with unashamed nepotistic bias; you couldn't hope for a better tenant blackbird than DWP has been. Unless of course you're a baby blackbird who can't stand snails.

Oct 5th

The two bluetits are still finding plenty of insects to eat among the ripe fruit on the apple and pear trees; it's still more of the bumper aphid breeding programme. This pair of birds has been around here a long time too.

Oct 6th

Yesterday I travelled to a farm in the South Downs National Park, volunteering to plant native trees as part of a rewilding project around the headwaters of our local river. While there I observed a massive and incredibly muscular bull standing in the next field; it stayed absolutely still through the whole time we were there. I had long wondered how animals like this can develop such amazing muscles just by standing in a field and eating grass. But then my Qi Gong teacher explained that this is a recognised technique in oriental martial arts; if you stand the right way it becomes strengthening and energising rather than tiring or weakening. He showed me how to do it, and I now use it whenever I'm standing in a queue. Wild animals such as buffalo, bison and musk ox have to be able to do this in order to be incredibly strong without doing press-ups, lifting weights or running around and burning precious calories - and it's crucial that they have that strength to fend off predators and protect their young.

When the work was finished the farmer pointed to a spot down by the river and told me he'd recently seen a puma there a couple of days in a row, eating a deer and in the end leaving nothing but bones and hooves. Now there's been all kinds of stories about big cats in UK and I've dismissed them all as mistaken identity by people who haven't a clue about animal identification. But this farmer was a reliable and down-to-earth chap who spoke about it in a matter-of-fact way, and I found myself believing him. Now that would be serious rewilding.

Oct 7th

After a couple of days of rain the seed feeder is out again and popular as ever with the small birds, today primarily sparrows and bluetits. These two species have completely different patterns of feeding there. The sparrows fight for a space on one of the perches and hold on to that as long as they can before they're bullied off by another sparrow, usually an alpha female.

The bluetits wait till there's no-one else on the perch, and even then they don't cling on to feed – they fly in, grab a seed and immediately fly off to a nearby perch to eat it. They're so fast you can't believe they got anything at all. These two species are each doing what works as part of their respective niche lifestyle.

Oct 8th

Bizarrely, two sparrows are carrying nesting material into the formerly-known-as-the-starlings' nestbox, which they've been using for a couple of years now. So I'm thinking: what, nesting again at this time of year, a bizarre effect of climate change? Or are they making a cosy roosting space for winter? Or an excuse for extra rumpy-pumpy? Hard to say.

Oct 9th

Unexpected events occur surprisingly often in the wild garden, such as examples of peaceful co-existence in what is in most respects a ruthlessly competitive realm. Today - as usual - sparrows are all over the feeder, dislodging lots of seeds which fall to the ground where a parent female woodpigeon is with two young twins. The youngsters are unsure what to do but are learning the trade from mum, who's demonstrating what a feeding frenzy looks like. At the same time one of the squirrel twins is foraging on the ground for those fallen seeds that have husks. I'd have thought this would cause conflict but it's all co-operative and tolerant.

Where feeding is concerned, conflict seems to be greater within rather than between species; a blackbird, for instance will see off another blackbird but quite happily share food on the ground with robins and sparrows. This can be explained by the fact that they each have their niche, and animals occupying a different niche from you are not a threat; in fact their presence can be welcome as it provides additional warning of imminent danger. Wildlife real estate is all about niche/niche/ niche. If you have a good niche in a good location you can survive and therefore it's worth defending with your life against your direct competitors.

Today's line-up is also surprising because squirrels are typically anxious about spending any time on the ground, but these particular youngsters didn't have the chance to learn to be flighty and terraphobic by their mom before she was whisked away; so they seem to be learning for themselves what is safe and what is dangerous. in this particular garden. They're certainly not as spooked by human proximity as grey squirrels normally are. But where is the other squirrel twin? I've not seen them apart terribly often. Has it wandered off, found someone it liked better, or been caught by a cat?

Oct 10th

Yesterday was traditionally the last day blackberries should be picked because today – the feast of old St Michaelmas - marks the day Lucifer got himself expelled from heaven for being a very naughty boy and certainly not a Messiah. He fell from the skies and landed in a spiky bramble bush. Understandably upset, he scorched the berries with his fiery breath, cursed them, stamped on them and for good measure spat all over them with his fevered saliva. You have been warned. And here's a thought: did Satan acquire his legendary over-heatedness through falling all that distance from heaven and through the Earth's atmosphere?

Oct 12th

Harmonious feeding is even more evident today, with still more diverse species feeding in the garden at the same time but still in their niche-distinctive ways.

The whole sparrow tribe are at the seed feeder. The wood pigeon trio are underneath, hoovering up everything they knock down to the ground, and the youngsters are learning fast. The female blackbird is turning over leaf mould to find worms, while a sozzled DWB is pecking at the fermenting windfall apples for his daily tipple of fruit alcohol. The squirrel is foraging all round the garden and carrying stuff off to the winter cache. The hyperactive wrens hop from branch to branch in the elder tree searching for invertebrates in the bark, while the pair of bluetits –keeping their distance from the sparrows - are finding insects in the tops of the fruit trees. There's still a great deal of mellow fruitfulness about.

Oct 14th

The twin squirrels have both been seen again, and are still functioning as a combination after all. They now appear to be building another drey for winter on top of the old alarm box in the tangle of evergreen clematis that covers the front wall of the house – right outside my study window – using a site where sparrows nested earlier. Mom definitely wouldn't have been comfortable within human sight from a much-used room. They're bringing in extra twigs, leaves. Moss, bits of bark and feathers. The smaller twin, probably the female - is living pretty much full-time within the garden: another indicator of this site's developing self-sufficient-system status.

Both squirrels are now gathering the fruiting and seed-bearing 'keys' from the ash tree that stands on the roadside outside our house, scurrying up and down the tree non-stop. When gathering winter food and moving it from gathering spot to store they always race like mad; either there's still some genetic trace of not wanting to be on the ground for too long, or they're worried someone else might grab the goods before they do - or maybe they think winter's starting tomorrow. Obviously they've never experienced the onset of winter before.

Seeing these twins develop together without parental guidance throws up some interesting questions about what is learned and what is innate among animals and other creatures. They've certainly learned to forage entirely without an example to follow, and now they know that before winter sets in they need to gather extra food, work out which items will have a long shelf life, and build a cold-proof home. There's a reason why we humans call this process 'squirreling stuff away'.

Oct 16th

Squirrels in the garden are making headlines again. A magpie has been watching closely and is now investigating the spot where they're storing their food

in their other drey - the ivy covered fork in the apple tree - when they're not there. I imagine the squirrels will be well capable of chasing off any magpie caught in the act of daylight robbery.

Oct 18th

Like all other fruits and berries in this mast year (explained in the diary entries for September) haws are hugely abundant this year. And they stay longer on the tree than just about any other berry, perhaps because they're the least delicious and therefore only eaten when there isn't much else. Flocks of Redwing can be seen eating them systematically at the tail end of winter, for instance, and native thrushes and blackbirds will take them too when there's nothing else. What is striking this year in particular is that, together with the huge numbers of these berries on each hawthorn bush, they're very brightly coloured and look sensational when caught in the low reddish autumn sunlight which further highlights their innate colour, so that the bushes just now are looking positively fluorescent. I've never seen this so evident in any previous year.

Haws have a tart and tangy taste, but without much flesh around their disproportionately large stone. They do however contain large amounts of antioxidants called polyphenols which have strong anti-inflammatory properties, said to help reduce high blood pressure and anxiety, guard against heart attack, reduce digestive problems and even prevent hair loss. I gather some each year, dry them and use through the winter. You don't see many thrushes with hair loss.

Oct 19th

The pair of bluetits is once again actively investigating the nestboxes and taking turns to look inside them even though breeding time is six months off. Are they one of those couples we all know who keep going to look at properties that are for sale even though they have no plans for moving anytime soon - "to see what's on the market", they say, but we all know they just want to get a look inside other people's homes when they're out?

Oct 21st

A wood-mouse is coming into the conservatory again looking for crumbs. This time it's at night time, but it's not at all bothered by the artificial light. This creature - with its cute little round body, big ears, huge eyes and very long tail – ranks high in the adorability stakes.

Oct 23rd

This morning a male pheasant of all things, in all his finery, walked all the way down our road, which is near the centre of town. The last time anyone living can remember seeing this happen was just after the Second World War, which was when these houses had just been built and the countryside was at the end of the street. That's biodiversity for you.

That evening I learned on the neighbourhood WhatsApp group that the pheasant was photographed in late afternoon at the railway station, which lies in the opposite direction from that in which it had been walking earlier. Obviously just a day tripper, now on its way home. Not keen on wasting energy flying then.

Oct 25th

I'm not much of a twitcher, but got excited today when a juvenile greater spotted woodpecker came to the garden. What made this extra special is that it was pecking for insects in the softer parts of the wild cherry tree – not eating peanuts at a bird feeder, which is what this species is more usually found doing in gardens.

Oct 27th

I carry out a quick survey of sparrow behaviour on the seed feeder to determine which individuals can hang on the longest there before being dislodged by others. This 'research lite' shows that juveniles get moved on the quickest and that adult males do better, but that the mature females are way the fiercest, turning round and stabbing anyone who tries to dislodge them. We all know people like that. The lowest status birds – though possibly the most savvy – enjoy the easier pickings spilled on the ground below the feeder by the battlers above. They don't get their pick of their favourite seeds but they get to eat continuously.

Oct 28th

There's been a mysterious biblical-plague scale hatch of blue-bottle flies in the house. Each time you go into certain rooms there are new ones. All flying at the windows, but they're not buzzing and have very slow reflexes - you can easily catch them in your hand - as if they're exhausted and haven't got long to live. I go round systematically opening windows to let them out, then closing the windows as soon as they're gone to prevent more coming in. But next time I go in that room there are others. What's going on?

Oct 29th

The blackbirds are still benefiting from windfall pears, which they prefer to those still on the tree. Each individual bird selects one pear at a time – the most perfect it can find - and keeps returning to that one until it's completely eaten, chasing off anyone else who tries to muscle in. Only when that perfect pear is completely finished will it move on to another. They seem to be looking for the perfect state of fermentation without mouldiness or mushiness; I've done checks and can confirm that those they favour exhibit the delicious fragrance of pear cider. And that's why they don't eat pears still in the tree. And that's why, with eating the fermenting apples too, they're mostly tipsy through autumn.

We've solved the mystery of the ever-increasing fly plague: a dead mouse under the floorboards.

Oct 30th

Another glorious Indian Summer day. The whole flock of sparrows is taking turns to bathe exuberantly in the bird bath, which is draped over now by branches bowed down by the extraordinary weight of this year's remaining pear crop. The birds seem to appreciate the security this cover offers.

The sparrows always bathe together - never as individuals, as blackbirds do - so that there's always somebody looking out in all possible directions. It's a noisy business, and perhaps on this one occasion the cheerful sounding din is actually expressing cheerfulness. They're surprisingly particular about water quality and won't bathe when there are fallen leaves or algae in the water, which makes sense as fresh water will carry less transmittable bird disease.

Oct 31st

The last cross-quarter day of the year, the Celtic festival of Samhain, the day and night of the betwixt and between, when the veil between the world of the physical and the world of spirit is at its thinnest and when revelations are possible.

I know this is wrong but I have to own up to still having a mental 'favourite species' list and another 'public enemies' list. of species frequenting the garden. And I've become aware that my rankings of species vary from time to time within each of these lists, so for objectivity I've drawn up a list of attributes for favoured species and for public enemy status to help me decide on difficult cases. Here they are:

Attributes for Favoured Species:

- Be cute, fetching or adorable
- Live as fully as possible on-site
- Get on well with other favoured species
- Have food preferences that leaves plenty available for others
- If at all possible, as icing on the cake, be a rare species

Attributes for Public Enemies:

- Eat all the food provided, leaving nothing for others
- Live elsewhere and only visit the garden opportunistically
- Terrorise, kill and eat members on the favoured species list
- Being numerous is a bonus in making this category

This is the sort of thing I find myself fretting over. Under 'public enemies', the magpies certainly occupy my number one spot, but who is #2: the carrion crows? The wood pigeons? The grey squirrels? And what about the seagulls? They all have their undesirable traits, but it's not a straightforward decision. And the sparrow-hawk is a real anomaly: kills and eats favoured species but is a charismatic, not-overly-numerous, top-of-the-food-chain species. A chap who takes his obsessive compulsions seriously could lose sleep over matters like this.

Take those squirrels for instance. At the start of this year, things were very clear for me: grey squirrels were Very Bad. But as I've seen the orphaned youngsters fending for themselves and not doing too much bad stuff, I've found myself evolving from hating them to tolerating them, to now being tempted to admit I may actually like them. They're winning me over with their curiosity, charm and relentless ability to overcome challenges. They're nearly always there, stubbornly getting through thick and thin, through lean times and times of plenty. How can I resent them, or wish they weren't there? They're creatures of innocence, and this garden has probably been the saving of them in their early days when they were orphaned and needed safety and readily obtainable food. I have to admit that baby grey squirrels have cuteness that can verge dangerously close to adorability. Where has my ruthless favouritism gone?

Perhaps what I'm feeling - from an evolutionary point of view, as ever – is that quasi-parenting affection: when you're part of what's making provision for young beings, and when they're 'in your care' for long enough, you can't help growing to love them; it's one of our inherited genetic traits. Maybe next year I'll love the carrion crows. Maybe a decade after that I'll love the magpies. I mean, all these creatures are innocent in a way, aren't they? How can I blame them for doing what they're suppose to do, and surviving against the odds? It's confusing.

So I've decided to quantify and evaluate the annoyingly unstable positions of species on my enemies list and my favourites list by drawing up some sort of matrix and assessing it periodically. Below is a sample: a graph where the horizontal axis represents likeability and the vertical axis nuisance value, showing current positioning for a few example species. Bottom right is most favourable position, top left is least:

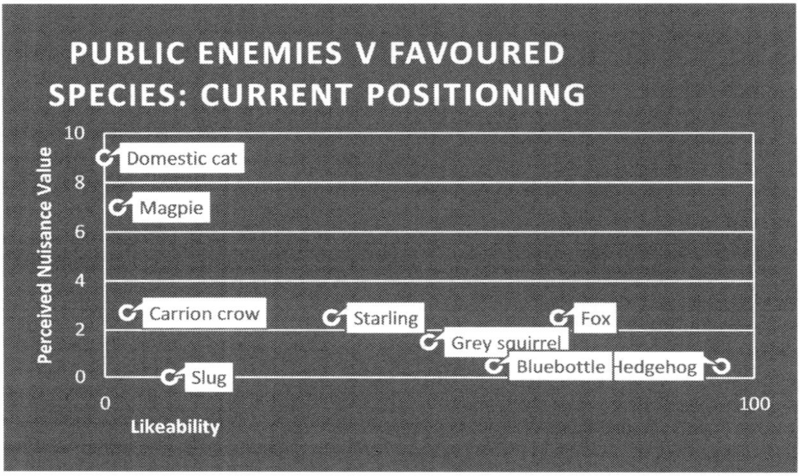

However, I see immediately that this graph represents only a partial picture because it ignores critical data for species that bring delight: they do so in proportion presence they have in the garden. The emperor dragonfly is amazing, but has only appeared once; sparrows are not stunningly beautiful, but they're there all the time, so cumulatively they bring huge pleasure.

I clearly a further matrix which sets how wonderful I reckon a creature is against how often I see it, thus expressing overall the total joy it brings. Here's a sample showing current positioning of a range of liked species. Top right positioning is highest score, bottom left lowest:

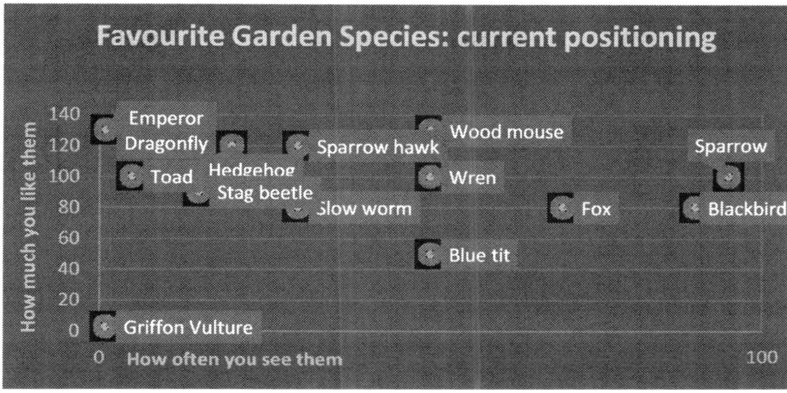

Oct 31st during the night:

Awakening from a disturbing dream probably arising from my previous day's un-conservation-minded outpouring, where I'm haunted by creatures I must decide whether I love or hate but have never seen before.

Confused, moi? Probablement.

November

Nov 1st

Observing the ants going about their business is always an interesting wild garden activity. At this time of year they're not out every day, but today is sunny and they're doing sorties round and about.

We could learn a thing or two from ants. They seem, for a start, to have ways of avoiding pandemics via an array of extraordinary and highly effective ways of preventing and dealing with outbreaks of viral infections in their extremely close-knit social communities. They employ antibacterial tree resins, for instance, in construction of their nests in the first place. They do social distancing as a matter of course, and limit contact between different ant groups such as workers/ foragers/ nurses. When an ant is ill with an infectious condition it will stay away from the nest. If an individual shows sign of illness at home they will spray it with formic acid; if it cannot be saved it will be killed and disinfected. Admittedly this latter point may be going a little too far for humanity.

Nov 3rd

Foxes are already uttering noisy mating calls by night, which is early for them. We've not got to the stage of hearing the full blood-curdling wailing scream of the vixen yet, but individuals are certainly letting each other know their location.

Once a pair starts mating they will continue to do so with each other every year until one of the two dies, and in that time they won't mate with other individuals. During the mating season the male of a pair will defend at any cost the female who will carry his genes forward; battles arising from this can be fatal.

Nov 6th

The sparrows' version of a dawn chorus – taking place well post-dawn – continues unabated even as autumn begins to turn into winter. It always starts with one bird who sets about waking everyone else up; in less than a minute the entire flock will be chattering at full volume, from within the foliage where they spent the night roosting. The birds can spend up to an hour on this activity in the morning, and repeat the whole thing in the late afternoon as they're settling down ahead of the coming night.

It seems to be the equivalent of starling's prolonged murmuration and rooks' playing in the sky before and after sleep, all of which are known to serve purposes of social bonding as well as exchanging practical information about feeding and other opportunities. Those flocking birds can afford this kind of luxury.

Repeatedly listening to this morning and evening ritual has shown me still further how me much I have underestimated the sparrow's range of vocal expression. Especially during the settling-down period I'm hearing sounds that can variously be described as squawky, screechy, ratchetty, guttural and gurgly – and all as raucous as usual. I guess I had been assuming these calls came from some other type of bird. It seems that the non-standard sounds – ie other than the stereotypical cheep-cheeps – are uttered when the birds are all hidden in cover, when more expansive communication is not such a security risk.

Nov 8th

There's been a terrific show of autumn leaf colour this year, and it's lasting for an unusually prolonged period. Yellow shades are prevalent, instigated by the native field maples back in October. Yellow and red pigments are in the leaves all year round but are obscured by the green supplied by chlorophyll until there isn't enough light or day length to sustain the latter; then we see the other colours.

This year we've experienced optimum conditions for a great show - mild autumn weather with sunny days and cool nights - but without the cold snap that would make the leaves drop quicker. No leaves seem to have fallen at all so far – very late, and very lovely to see.

Deciduous trees have been dropping their leaves seasonally for 100 million years, so there must be benefits in following this seemingly wasteful pattern rather than conserving resources. Actually, all trees drop individual leaves when they've outlived their effective lives, but broad-leaved deciduous trees do so on a regular yearly basis and all at one go while evergreens do it more gradually and continuously. The deciduous approach - doing it comprehensively and in one go – brings advantages. These include conserving resources through winter, avoiding presence of moisture in leaves that would freeze winter; and protecting against wind damage to branches - or indeed whole trees - when the leaf area catches stormy winter winds.

Evergreen trees - mostly conifers - take other measures to prevent these effects. In particular, they have narrow leaves or needles with a waxy coating and a compact conical overall tree structure that throws off rain and snow and catches less wind, which is particularly effective in more extreme latitudes where winters are harshest and snowfalls heaviest. Horses for courses.

Nov 11th

As the sun starts to go down at 4pm I see a single adolescent squirrel playing by itself in the high foliage, racing round madly and leaping from tree to tree; I've only previously seen this when it was with its twin sibling. At this time of year it's hard not to see this as some sort of joie-de-vivre display. It's also hard not to find it endearing: it's a welcome prompt to joy as winter approaches.

I'm coming round to the opinion that grey squirrels aren't as harmful in a wild garden as they would be in a more highly cultivated bare-earth eco-system. After all, they can't dig up your bulbs if you don't plant any; they can't eat your seeds if you're not sowing any; they can't eat your crops if you haven't got any. The wilder trees and shrubs are probably more tolerant of a little bark-eating than cultivated varieties. And squirrels can't make holes in your beautifully manicured lawn if there is no lawn.

In a properly wild garden where supplementary food is also provided for the birds they can find all the food they need without damaging the order of things. They live, in fact, more like squirrels would live in the wild. And they haven't needed to get in our roof-space – another common worry with squirrels - because they can build perfectly good nests in the dense tree cover afforded outdoors here.

Nov 14th

The hen blackbird is gorging herself on the profuse orange berries of Pyracantha (or Firethorn). It isn't truly native as are most of the shrub species in this garden, but it was already here before we arrived and it has a lot of wildlife appeal: those berries that all the thrush family love, masses of white blossom in spring that provides nectar for hosts of flying insects, and the worst thorns you'll find on any shrub, which makes is great for nesting in and hiding from predators.

Nov 16th

Speaking of predators and hiding from them, looking out of my office window I see a sparrow-hawk perched right outside, gazing at me with its fiercely piercing brilliant orange eyes. Every bird has vanished. Not enjoying having its gaze returned, it flies off. I wonder what it was after? Anything with wings, probably.

Nov 19th

It's pouring with rain. I put the bird seed feeder in shelter of the house porch so that the birds can source dry seed there; it's often accessed by sparrows. But now I see a wood-mouse scurrying back and forth between the feeder and the woodpile where it lives, building up its winter larder, even in daylight. I guess it knows that dry seed keeps better. I built the woodpile for hedgehogs but they haven't occupied it; so now it's being used in this unplanned way, and the hedgehogs have been attracted by other

resources here. It just goes to show that you can create wildlife opportunities, but you can't tell how or by whom they will be taken up. So multi-purpose solutions perform best.

Nov 21st

Extraordinarily, leaves are still on the branches and now all shades of spectacular autumn colour are still to be enjoyed on the trees this year, from green to yellow to red and brown. Most spectacular in the garden is the hazel tree whose every leaf is vivid golden yellow: another dose of joy and transcendence.

Sparrow pairs are fighting over the SparrowCam nestbox that was so very popular from March into June – but this is late November. Must be a dream home by sparrow real estate criteria.

Nov 24th

A pair of woodpigeons is sitting on the fence. The male suddenly jumps onto the female, flaps his wings, does his bit and hops back down onto the fence. The female tries to cuddle up to him but he moves away and sits with his head turned away from her. She turns her head away from him. They both continue to sit there for a long time, hunching up their bodies and both looking away from each other like they're sulking. We've all been there.

I always wonder how sincere is the male woodpigeon's courting habit of deeply bowing in front of the female, which seems to say "I humbly and profoundly respect you/ I would never ever be interested in any other female/ I will be yours forever/ I will be the very model of devotion, if you will only accept me unworthy as I am." Yeah, right.

Nov 25th

Suddenly there are three squirrels in the garden at once, chasing each other round like mad. One falls from the top of a tree all the way to the ground; I've never seen a squirrel lose its grip like that. It seems to be fine; the ground is damp, soft and covered everywhere in fallen, decaying foliage.

Are the two siblings who've been here all year over-excited about a newcomer? Is this early flirtation in advance of mating in the new year? Or are they just having fun? Send your answers on a postcard please.

Nov 27th

Another huge buzz of honey-bees all over ivy blossom, in a different corner from that observed last month. The flowers of the ivy bushes seem to peak at different times in different parts of the garden due to varying aspect and local micro-climatic conditions. This is a fortunate arrangement both for the ivy plants - who are therefore not competing with one another - and for the invertebrates who get a longer season of nectar and pollen availability.

Nov 28th

The male song-thrush is living up to his name. Why does he sing so vigorously first thing every morning at this time of year, when no female will be thinking about mating until the other side of winter? Well, it's to retain his territory and its food sources, not from rival local birds but from other non-indigenous mistle- and song-thrushes arriving from Scandinavia hoping to escape the harsh winter there and establish a fruitful winter territory over here. While our bird is singing with such commitment here, they're going to have to look elsewhere.

Nov 30th

The sloes are nearly ripe enough to eat now; I can tell because visiting Redwings are guarding them from other birds. These birds can tell when they are ripening without tasting them. How? It's all about a special type of vision they possess.

Discovering how very differently sight and vision work in different creatures opens up much greater understanding: what they do, how their lives work, and how they manage in the ceaseless struggle of life, death and reproduction; finding things to eat and avoiding getting eaten.

The world as seen by other species is hugely different from what we see. No creature, in fact, sees everything objectively as it really is; all species 'see' a selective and subjective interpretation of data according to what suits their particular needs. And sight varies in many different ways.

Let's take the number and positioning of eyes, for a start. Generally speaking, predators have evolved forward-looking eyes and will look straight ahead, whereas prey species' eyes are positioned to the side of the head, so they look at you sideways. That's why so many animals are freaked out when humans peer at them – we've got forward-looking eyes and they will assume we're eyeing them up for a meal. Predators also have generally developed vision that's best for focusing on a single target, usually with eyes close together like ours, which gives good depth perception and judgement of distance; birds of prey can see their target three kilometres away. Prey species develop a wider field of vision that is also hypersensitive to detecting movement. Horses, for instance, see two separate images, one from each eye, and have a blind spot right in front of their noses; humans use brain processing to merge the images from our two eyes into one integrated picture. Mice – another variation - can move each eye independently of the other; they see two different images; but their vision is somewhat blurred so they're mainly aware of the overall movement of shapes. Crocodiles, too, can't see detail; that's why you see them throwing themselves at the silhouette of a wildebeest and snapping at whatever bit happens to be within range.

Numbers of eyes can vary greatly. Mammals, birds and fish have two eyes whereas spiders have eight pairs, giving full peripheral vision. Flies have thousands of tiny eyes, which is why they're so difficult to swat.

But differing perception of colour is probably where the most striking differences between species occurs; understanding this can open up a whole new world of insight into the way wild creatures operate. We all see something by way of light reflected off it, and different colours of light vibrate at very different wavelengths and frequencies. There's a middle range of colours, and then there's ultraviolet at the shorter wavelength of the spectrum and infrared at the longer end. The number of colour pigments any creature can detect is determined by the range of receptors it has in its eyes. Humans can only distinguish three pigments - red, yellow and blue - so we have a relatively narrow and selective band of sensitivity; in fact we believe these are the 'primary' colours, which they are only for us, not in reality. In the animal world this makes us the odd ones out. It's thought that human vision evolved to be optimal for detecting the colour of ripening fruit, way back in the days when we lived among the treetops.

Dogs have even less colour range than we do; their vision is virtually monochromatic; but they see well in the dark, and their acute sense of smell makes up for visual shortcomings. Foxes are broadly the same, having a low-resolution visual system overall, but with good visual acuity at short range – you could say that they're short-sighted - and with extreme sensitivity to movement at any range. The downside is that they're very poor at detecting objects which don't move, which is why rabbits freeze when hunted by them, producing the 'rabbit in the headlights' scenario; cars were not around when rabbits evolved this otherwise effective response. Another specialised feature possessed by foxes is that, like cats, they have vertically-slit pupils which help them adapt their vision to a wide range of light levels, from the brightest sunlight right down to near darkness. This feature is probably why we think they look so cunning. Additionally, their retina has internal reflectivity, so that light entering the eye from an object is reflected back again around the eye; this too greatly enhances low-light vision. It also explains why the fox's eye reflects back light from your torch so vividly, usually but not always looking green to us.

Overall, though, the fox's superb hearing is thought to be its most important sense, followed by sight and only then smell. There is another superpower, though; foxes, (and also dogs and mice) have 'magneto reception': they can see the worlds' geomagnetic field and locate magnetic North wherever they are, which helps them accurately measure distance between themselves and prey. That's why a dog can find its way home across a continent. Foxes really are amazingly adaptable creatures, which continue to do well even in the closest proximity to human beings..

Birds in general have very sharp vision but poor hearing and smell. Pigeons can see millions of different hues and have better colour vision than most other animals. I've no idea why they should need this, but maybe it's one of the things that helped them become the highly versatile and successful species they are worldwide. Nocturnal animals like geckos are three hundred and fifty times more sensitive to colour at night than we are. Snails can't focus or see colour, but can detect different intensities of light which is how they know to hide in dark places in the daytime and come out to party at night. Many insects pick up very wide ranges of colour pigments; the champion is dragonfly which has up to thirty, meaning that they can distinguish many millions of colour variations.

But among colours, being able to detect ultraviolet - which of course we can't - is the big game-changer. Are you old enough to remember UV lighting at discos in the 70s, when everyone wore white to look purple, and everybody thought this was a good look for attracting a mate?

Most other animals can detect UV reflectance. This serves a number of different purposes, according to species. The most immediate application is in foraging and finding food. UV light, it turns out, is reflected off many berries and flowers to advertise themselves as being ripe or having nectar, in order to spread their seeds or get pollinated. This is what our Redwings are doing; the sloes develop a waxy coating containing UV reflectant when they're ripe, so the birds can see this from a distance – and at night, which is when they travel, high overhead. The arrangement is good for the sloe bush too: it doesn't want the fruit to be eaten before the seed inside has fully ripened.

Bees, butterflies and other insects use UV reflectance as a prime way of finding sources of nectar and of pollen. As the outside membrane of many invertebrates also reflects UV, this helps UV-seeing birds and animals find and prey on them. Hawks such as kestrels can detect trails used by rodent prey because their urine leaves traces of UV.

The second application of UV pigmentation and ability to detect it is signalling, which is usually within the same species, used for general messaging and in particular for choosing or being chosen as a mate. Many birds have UV elements in their plumage, which means we have no idea how beautiful and attractive they really look. Which might explain why those of us who were of clubbing age in the 1970s thought wearing clothing that picked up the fashionable ultra-violet lighting then would be good for mate attraction. It didn't work for me but that was probably because I wasn't good mating material.

The third element in animal vision is about orientation and navigation in the world. UV light is a component of the atmosphere and is all around us, particularly evident at dawn and dusk when the sun's angle is low. It also varies in intensity with different landscapes such as mountains or oceans and in relation to the poles and the Earth's axis, so is hugely helpful for migrating species such as geese or seabirds. Even dogs use their UV vision to orientate themselves around their territory as well as in new places.

Finally, there's the infrared end of the light spectrum. A limited number of predators such as snakes and mosquitoes have evolved capacity to detect this in order to home in on body heat emitted by prey, especially at night. This is particularly beneficial to snake species which generally have poor vision and really only see movement.

So humans have managed to survive with limited sight potential compared with most other creatures, and we haven't even got particularly acute other senses. Indeed, today nearly half of Americans are short-sighted; in normal evolutionary circumstances they would have quickly starved or been eaten. Animals in nature cannot afford this luxury; they don't normally live long enough to experience age-related vision deterioration, or indeed age-related anything. Those with vision impairment don't pass their genes on – like ancient humans who had myopia. Where the human race is most short-sighted, of course, is in relation to our effects at a planetary level.

And the colours we 'see' are subjective and just part of the picture; so - contrary to romantic assertions in the well-known Valentine message - Roses aren't really red/ violets aren't actually blue/ though sugar is decidedly sweet/ and on a case-by-basis so are potentially you. We're just wrong in our understanding of so many things.

Kill-joie, moi? Non - realistique.

December

Dec 1st

First day of meteorological winter in the northern hemisphere. The sparrows' noisy waking chatter continues, even at the end of a very cold winter's night. It sounds so enthusiastic, like "Wow, amazing, we've survived another night!"

Dec 2nd

The goldfinches are a joy, too, with their exotic colouring and charming ways. They're loving the Nyjer seed feeder I put out for them recently, which has tiny feeding holes through which only these finches can get their very narrow beaks. These have been evolved to pull out the very small thistle seeds on which they live all year - only in spring do they find insects to feed their young - hence the old Saxon name *thisteltuige* or thistle-tweaker. The males, with slightly longer beaks, can also eat the seeds of teasels but the females can't. What would be the evolutionary reason for this? Maybe the teasel seeds contain some nutrient that's good for male finch hormones. These delightful birds also love hulled sunflower seeds. Unlike insectivorous birds, they need to constantly drink water as their diet is completely dry.

Goldfinches are more timid and also more patient than sparrows. They will only eat when everything is quiet in the garden, and these ones never fight over the feeding opportunity – perhaps because they're a single family group and therefore have an established hierarchy. In larger flocks they can be more quarrelsome.

The wild goldfinch was on the brink of extinction in Britain in the early twentieth century because of its popularity as a colourful cage bird, but the RSPB managed to persuade the UK government to ban all caging of wild birds in 1933. Numbers have since been greatly helped by the growing popularity of garden feeding, as the bird is tolerant of being around humans.

Dec 3rd

A milder day today, with the ground softer. The long-standing resident blackbird DWB takes the opportunity to search for worms, and is still doing so as dusk falls. Blackbirds seem to feed longer and sing later than most other garden birds apart from that frequent nocturnal vocalist, the robin.

Dec 4th

There are still bright yellow leaves left from autumn on the hazel bush. Honeysuckle is blossoming again in some parts of the garden; I believe I've seen it in bloom in every month of this year. That wasn't so when I was a lad, before climate change was even a twinkle in a fossil fuel magnate's eye.

Dec 5th

The weather has turned cold again and looks set to rain all day. I've added the suet block cage for the birds to feed on; not only does suet provide the birds with more intensive and instant fat reserves, but they're happy to feed on it in heavy rain as it's inherently water repellent, unlike seed in the feeder which quickly soak up the rain and get soggy.

The sparrows are on the suet block in the blink of an eye, even though all wild birds are usually wary of change. These sparrows know the fat block and they know they love it so they're soon squabbling all over it. Each block has six faces, so up to eight of them can attach to it at a time, including those clinging to the underside.

Starlings will also feed on the suet; I'll tolerate one or two but once a flock descends I take it back inside as they would devour the whole in half a minute. Full-time garden residents get unashamed preference here, and those first two are locals.

Dec 6th

Weather is colder still. A single goldfinch, an adolescent without full colouring, is at the Nyjer feeder. Then snow begins to fall. The bird stops feeding but stays on the perch, gazing all round, looking bewildered and wondering what's going on. It won't have seen snow before as it was born last spring and this is the first snow in our part of the country.

Eventually the juvenile resumes feeding, but stops every now again to look at the snow as if to say, "What is this stuff? Is it dangerous?" I've never seen a goldfinch keep so still for so long; they're usually flighty birds. Delightful and charming, hence the collective name for this bird.

Dec 8th

One of the sparrow-hawks made a brief appearance today but didn't catch anything. This was the female, who visits more often at this time of year than in the breeding season when she is constantly on the nest. There's a striking size difference between the male and female; she can be heavier than him by half his weight or even more.

There's always an evolutionary reason for everything in nature, and the varying relative size of males and females of different species provides a fascinating example. In humans the male is on average 8% taller than the female, and 20% heavier. With most bird species, too, the males are larger, especially where they compete for food with the females. Elephant seal males can be eight times heavier than the female; this is because the females don't do fighting and the males do. And in cichlid fish species the male can be sixty times larger than the female; they still manage to reproduce okay.

I find it interesting to compare this with other cases where the female is larger than the male. In bird species this tends to be either where the female mates with more than one male, or where we're talking about owls and raptors. This size differentiation is thought to be so that the two genders can hunt different prey sizes and varieties, so that as a couple they widen their food base – in effect giving the pair access to two different niches. It also means that the male, who spends much more time hunting, can catch the smaller prey which are more abundant and which range over more varieties than larger prey items. This size difference is especially true in raptors such as the sparrow-hawk which specialises in hunting fast, agile prey in confined spaces. The larger female size also supports greater egg production, and, I believe, reduces the male's temptation to eat the young if food is critically scarce.

In some bird species the greater size of the female is even more pronounced, such as in the Great Bustard; in this species the male is huge and the female is three times huger. Indeed, in species other than mammals and birds it's far more common for the female to be bigger, often a lot bigger. This includes most reptiles and amphibians, the vast majority of insects, almost all parasitic creatures and just about all wormy critters.

Female spiders are famously up to 100 times larger than the male, whom they refer to amongst themselves as being 'snack size'. As a result, males with the urge to mate will often choose a female who has just eaten, or indeed engage in mating while she is presently eating another male. We've all been there.

Other species go still further in the big-female stakes. Blanket octopus females can be 40.000 times heavier than the male; but the record is probably held by the Giant Sea-devil fish where she is 500,000 times bigger than he is. How does that work? One imagines that the name Giant Sea-devil may derive from how he refers to her with his mates in the pub.

Dec 10th

Weather still cold. The suet block in its hanging cage has brought out a family of three bluetits; that seems like the very small family group that we noted earlier in the season. Or is it from a different and bigger brood where all youngsters have departed except this one stay-with-mum-and-dad teen?

The robin is feeding from the suet block too – you don't see that on the seed feeder; he's usually a ground feeder, not usually a 'clinger' like the sparrows or bluetits. The concentrated source of warming fat is just too tempting.

Dec 12th

The squirrel has worked out how to get at the suet cage hanging from a tree. Squirrels have a habit of knocking metal feeders to the ground and then gnawing them apart to get at what's inside all in one go, so I've worked out a solution: tie a cord between two trees and hang the block halfway along. Seems to work so far. Squirrel has not yet learned tight-rope walking, but watch this space.

Dec 13th

The robin is still singing: our only British bird to hold its territory all year round. It's particularly lovely to hear it as darkness falls, prompted by the street lights coming on when paradoxically it goes into its dawn song. This is a common reflex in robins, which can often be heard singing in the middle of the night. The winter song is more subdued than the spring version.

Motivation to hold this little patch in the depths of winter – with the attendant risk of predation, usage of energy, and potential fights with rivals - is a further confirmation that it's a good feeding and nesting territory to which it will be confident about being able to attract a female in spring.

Both male and female robins generally sing from concealed positions, high in a tree; being easily visible would mean being a self-advertising target for a predator. For a brief period, in mid-winter only, already paired male and female robins can be seen feeding alongside one another. When new year comes, though, this peace agreement ends; yet the engagement is still there and they will reunite to make a family in spring. They're the fierce on-again/off-again Liz-Taylor-and-Richard-Burton couple of the bird world.

Dec 14th

Today, something I've never ever spotted before: a one-legged sparrow, managing to survive. It can stand on one leg; it can hop from perch to perch and grip the seed feeder as well as feeding on the ground; and it can presumably roost on one leg too. It may have been unsuccessfully caught by a sparrow-hawk who only got a foot for its trouble. I'm impressed.

Dec 15th

Woodpigeons are gobbling the ivy berries; I haven't seen that before, but then WPs are greedy omnivores. The ever possessive blackbirds will not be best pleased to see their late-winter reserves depleted, but WPs are too big to see off

Dec 16th

The squirrel we're seeing mostly on its own again now is having another round of mad leaping acrobatics through the foliage. It's extraordinarily agile and seems to be seeing how far it can leap without falling off.

Any brown that was mixed in with its predominantly grey colouring seems to be fading, with its tummy, ears and feet now completely white and the rest of its fur heading that way. Is this because there would now be complete snow cover in its native north America, and it would need the camouflage? It regularly comes to sit on my upstairs office window; I'm looking at it now as I write. It's peering back at me with apparent curiosity – a far cry from its hyper-fearful mother.

Dec 18th

The wood-mouse is poking around at a small hole in the ground that looks like an entrance for some small creature or other. The clue as to what may be going on here is that wood-mice eat hibernating queen bumblebees in winter if they can find them.

Dec 21st

Winter Solstice in the northern hemisphere: the point when darkness stops darkening and light starts lightening, and the festival borrowed from the Pagans by Christianity to rebrand its top offering, Christmas.

This is the time of year to start thinking again about our Big Prune. The trees and shrubs are generally let grow wild, but growth is so fast and furious in this extraordinarily fecund eco-system – everything grows upwards by a couple of metres each year - that they need to be cut back annually at the tops. In a truly wild place, of course, limiting growth would be done by wild herbivores. So a rewilder needs to step in to fill this role or the whole garden will turn into dense, dark impenetrable jungle in very few years.

It's also the time for bringing in a festive holly bough laden with red berries. This is what people did before Christmas and Christmas trees were invented. This is an altogether more eco-friendly solution than the popular commercial one; in the new year it will go back into the garden to decay and support new life. On my Facebook page the idea gets a lot of likes and prompts imitation.

Dec 24th

The easterly wind is so cold this morning that the sparrows are staying in their weatherproofed roosting shrubs a couple of hours later than usual, even though both seed feeder and suet block are available.

Later in the morning the wind direction changes but keeps blowing. Food is out on the hanging feeder, but all the birds are reluctant to take any. This is because every piece of foliage in the garden is moving and they're programmed to be hyper-wary of such movements which would signify danger. Eventually a few sparrows feed a little, but very tentatively, looking around them continuously between pecks, which is untypical of their flock feeding patterns. The hungrier they are, the more prepared they have to become to take calculated risks; they know they need to put on the brown fat to get through the night. In the end, though, they all they stop feeding even though there's still food left.

Dec 25th

The squirrels are not picking the last of the unpicked small apples off the tree and taking them away to store in their winter drey, That seems to be all they want for Christmas.

Dec 27th

Christmas festivities are over – and so is a big storm which blew through the land yesterday, wreaking damage and floods everywhere. But not in this garden; the high surrounding hedge, strengthened throughout by dense tangles of honeysuckle and ivy, remains undamaged, and has provided calm shelter throughout for all the resident birds and mammals.

Dec 29th

The squirrel is tucking into holly berries – not part of its usual job description - but then this one grew up without parental guidance. Maybe it'll end up with an upset tummy. Going about this task methodically, it goes to a twig, reaches out, picks a single berry, takes it back to a safe branch, eats it there, then returns for another, and repeats. So sweet.

Observing this dedicated procedure is a clincher for me; today I pronounce that the squirrel has officially moved off my public enemy list and onto the preferred species list - with the privileges this brings, of which it will no doubt be blissfully unaware.

Dec 31st

This calendar year is coming to an end; who knows what world events are coming down the line, and what difference they will make to the denizens of the wildlife garden?

The great thing to me is that everything that is in the garden – including just about every plant - has freely chosen to be here rather than somewhere else. Isn't that wonderful? My life has become so closely tied up with that of the garden residents and visitors; I know them all intimately, and they know me; we're all part of the same eco-system.

Looking back, I feel incredibly fortunate. This little world has given me so much over the course of the year, with all the differences in the seasons and the months: the August-ness of August, the May-ness of May. The big gifts? They are many: the feeling of being at least a part of the global solution rather than the problem; sharing the benefits of the garden with the local community; mental and emotional wellbeing and personal transformation; elevation of the spirits and forgetting for a while one's own worldly woes; answering long-held questions and gaining a deeper understanding of the magic of nature's extraordinary intricate web; reconnection with one's own inner wildness; cultivation of the helpful ability to live deeply in the infinite present; and a sense of joyful interconnectedness and ecstasy which at times is truly transcendental. I know these beings intimately, they know me and I know their children. I've enjoyed the continuous detective work of seeing who's doing what, and finding answers to the often complex questions of why. Plus, the journey has helped me come to terms with – perhaps even celebrate – by own shortcomings.

At its core, in fact, the year's journey with these myriad beings has been about the transcendental power of love. For me this journey, which has included preferred species lists and public enemy lists, has gone from definitely resenting some of them, to tolerating, to grudgingly admitting they're okay, to finally loving them – maybe even all of them: the sparrows, the hedgehogs, and the woodmice; the trees and shrubs and the other plants; the stag beetles, slow worms, frogs and toads; the butterflies and earwigs and woodlice and a thousand other invertebrates; the fungi, mycorrhizae bacteria and a trillion other microscopic and sub-microscopic beings; and maybe also the grey squirrels, the carrion crows and the magpies. What? Yes, maybe even the magpies. It's a work in progress.

Soppy, moi? Pourquoi non?

Thanks for joining me on this journey. May you have access to wildness forever.

The power of urban wildlife gardening

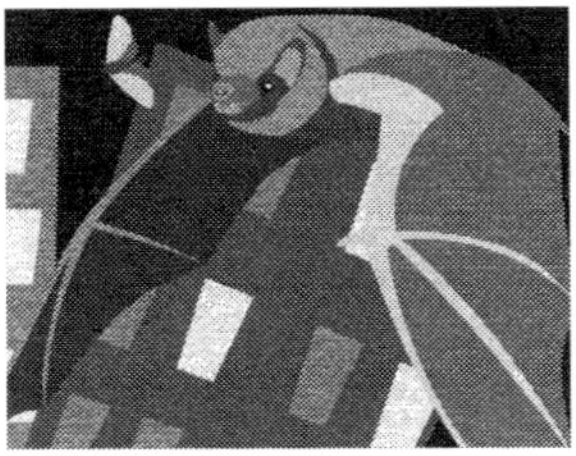

Urban wildlife gardening can bring tremendous benefits to you, to your local wildlife, to the quality of life in towns and cities, and to the planet. And it's not hard to do.

There's huge potential here. Domestic gardens constitute a very significant part of the urban landscape, forming a quarter of the total area of many cities. They can also represent half of urban green space. In countries like UK, more than 85% of the population lives in towns and cities; in the US it's 82%; worldwide it's currently 50 to 60% having risen from 34% in 1960, and is projected to reach 68% by 2050. We're becoming an urban species.

Scaled up urban wildlife gardening could play a tremendous role in turning the tide of urban development and reversing the inexorable concreting over of valuable small green spaces, making a direct and significant contribution to addressing global issues of over-development, pollution, climate change and species extinction.

Conventional gardening doesn't do that job nearly so well. It contributes significantly to ever rising carbon emissions through using and transporting horticultural products, chemicals, power tools, and plastics and other petroleum based materials, as well as supporting actions like destroying natural peat bogs in order to have potting compost. Addiction to perfectly manicured lawns represents the peak of this disastrous scenario. Wildlife gardens, on the other hand, are extremely significant carbon sinks. Regular gardens also use massive amounts of water, increasingly so as the effects of climate change are felt and water inevitably becomes a more and more scarce commodity. By contrast, established wild gardens use no extra water at all, and also soak up surplus water and thus help prevent flooding when there is excessive rainfall—which we're also going to see more of in many places.

Many declining wildlife species that were once common in the traditionally farmed countryside are now more abundant in urban areas because of the gardens there; in Europe examples include hedgehogs, frogs and song thrushes. Connecting with nature and wildness has been shown by a plethora of studies to benefit human mental and emotional wellbeing and overall health. And those studies show that having an urban wildlife garden bring these benefits too. Having even a small urban wild garden brings much of the appeal of the countryside into urban life.

Wouldn't it be wonderful if lots of urban gardeners decided to rewild at least a part of their gardens? This would have a huge beneficial impact on the ability of all kinds of wildlife to

survive and thrive in our towns, cities and suburbs, creating a network of wildlife corridors that connect with each other and with the surrounding countryside. Connectedness– rather than just creating isolated pockets of wildness– is now being recognised as the key way to execute conservation, as it enables vulnerable species to move when their original habitat becomes unsuitable as climate change effects kick in.
As renowned nature writer Mark Cocker says of this book: "If all of us did what the author's family are doing, we could scale up from a few, to many, to all gardens. Then we would revitalise something like 2 million acres of very important habitat. No plot is too small for you to change the world."

Wilding the urban garden, then, can make a huge difference – especially if a lot of us do it. So let's do something different with those arid bare-earth flowerbeds; let's go a bit mad with those manicured lawns; let's convert some of those hard-standings and concrete slabs into something more diversity-encouraging and fecund. A wild urban garden can be your own little eco-system and nature reserve. A lot of it is just getting out of the way and letting nature do its thing. You'll be surprised at just how many creatures appear in your vicinity when you let the habitat go wild and free. Let's do this!

Creating your own urban wildlife garden

The day-to-day contents of this book can support you if you decide you'd like to set up their own wildlife haven. No matter how small an outdoor space you have available, you will naturally attract all manner of exciting birds, animals, insects and plant species – and reap all those other rewards too.

Wilding your urban garden needn't be an all-or-nothing thing; you can take it as far as you wish, or have a hybridised garden that includes conventional elements such as flower or vegetable beds. Or you can proceed with wilding step by step over a period of years. It will still bring benefits.

You can create a rewarding and transformative connexion with nature and wildlife in even the most modest of gardens, even if it's a small patio or just a window box. And you can begin to get results quickly.

The fact is that turning a regular garden into a wildlife haven is not so much about doing stuff as it is about *not* doing stuff: not constantly tidying the place up, not dead-heading flowers when they've over, not planting new stuff, not weeding, hoeing or digging up beds. It's mostly about getting out of the way and letting nature take its course, which it will do speedily and powerfully if permitted. It's a natural process of reversion, which is what nature is perpetually trying to do.

For many people this means getting away from the traditional and quasi-moralistic idea that a garden must be neat and tidy and orderly or your neighbours will think you're a terrible person. It's a reversal of that oft quoted dictum from the *Field of Dreams* movie: if you *don't* build it, they will come; they will naturally be attracted to your plot in preference to more sterile gardens around you.

Wild plants (aka weeds) spread very quickly: remember how hard you have to work to keep them at bay? They have incredible vitality, so that plants which are present already or which have circulated seed will quickly invade bare earth, which nature abhors because it's not an efficient way to work. New plants will miraculously arrive, from seed blown in by the wind or via the digestive systems of bird and mammals.

So nature is going to do 95-99% of the work for you; but the other 1-5%, where you take some constructive measures, can also make a big difference. Such measures can greatly speed up the transition to wildness, increase the abundance and diversity of the plant and creature species, and make the garden a little more like you as an individual would like it to be. But keep it simple.

So here are my ten top-tip suggestions for measures you can take to facilitate the transition to wildness, while still leaving overall control to natural forces and letting species exercise their own choice. Some of these measures take effect quickly while others need a bit more time to bring their full effect. Take your pick.

10 Steps you can take

1 Let at least some areas of the garden go completely wild. Let grass grow long and don't worry if other plants invade it. Let, leaves, fallen twigs and dead plant material accumulate. Make habitats for invertebrates and other creatures by putting in log piles, leaf piles, compost heaps, and those insect hotels made out of hollow sticks which you can make or buy; some people make a 'city' version out of stacked pallets stuffed with a variety of hollow bits and pieces.

2 One of the best things you can do is establish a small pond if you haven't one already. You can buy small prefabricated ponds from garden centres; make sure you get one with a shallow ramp at one end so that amphibians and other creatures can easily get in and out. Put some aquatic plants in, but leave two thirds of the pond as open water. You will be amazed at how quickly aquatic insects, frogs, newts and toads may find their way to your pond, and non-aquatic creatures will be able

to drink from it or find food therein. Avoid all-day sun or deep shade for the pond's position.

If you can't manage a pond then provide water for creatures to drink and splash in, such as a birdbath.

3 Provide some food for birds and other creatures, according to season. Your wilding garden will gradually provide more and more natural food resources, but supplementing food will speed things up and help creatures get through the toughest seasons. Good quality mixed bird seed in tough feeders is an obvious choice, with an option of fat or suet blocks for very cold weather; choose mixes that cater for a wide range of species. Food can also be provided as appropriate for mammals such as hedgehogs. Remember that once you start feeding, the creatures will build this into their way of surviving and will be dependent on it when times are hard, so whatever level of support to provide, do it consistently. It's also important to make sure water is available all year round.

4 You don't have to add plant species; but if you do, I recommend native species over non-native, as they naturally attract and support much more local native wildlife.. Remember, for instance, that single flowering plants provide nectar for insects that double-flowering species don't.

5 Shrubs and small trees can play an extremely valuable role in even a small wildlife garden, especially if they provide dense cover for birds to hide, roost and nest in, and if they provide food such as berries and flowers. They can also offer food and shelter for a great range of insects and animals.

My suggestion, if you're adding shrubs, is to create a segment of hedgerow, which is the ultimate resource for wildlife, to complement open areas like a woodland glade. If you're buying shrubs and small trees, buy them as mature as you can so that they will establish a mature habitat quickly. You'll find that they grow at an extraordinary rate in the naturally fertile setting of a wild eco-garden. The ultimate hedge will have climbing plants growing through the shrubs, providing a dense protective canopy.

As with other plants, I suggest you prefer native species; and provide as great a variety as you can, just like you'd find in a wild hedgerow. You can plant out in winter if they're bare-rooted, but any time of year if in a pot. Here are my suggested top species for habitat creation and natural food provision in a European garden:

Shrubs and small trees:

Hawthorn; Holly; Elder; Hazel; Blackthorn; Rowan; Field Maple; Guelder Rose; Wild Cherry; Crab Apple; Goat Willow

Climbers:

Honeysuckle; Ivy; Blackberry aka bramble; Wild Rose

6 Provide nestboxes. These vary greatly in size of box and means of access and are each designed for specific species, so work out which type of birds are in your area and provide for those. Late winter is a good time to put up nestboxes so that the birds get used to them before claiming them to help attract a mate.

7 If you want to encourage hedgehogs to visit your garden and there isn't ready access available, make a 12cm square gap at the bottom of your fence. See if you can persuade adjacent neighbours to do the same, to create a neighbourhood hedgehog highway. Gardens are becoming the key habitat for this endearing and increasingly rare species as other habitats diminish. Gardens are also safer for them.

8 Get a trailcam – you'll be amazed at who is coming to visit your garden throughout the night. Cameras inside nest boxes are great too.

9 Start observing immediately. Either sit still for a while in the garden or watch from a window, and different things will be happening at different times of day and seasons. Notice how much better your new connexion with nature makes you feel.

10. Encourage children to visit your garden and learn about wildlife – its future depends on people in the future caring about it.

So let's do something different with those arid bare-earth beds; let's go a bit mad with those manicured lawns; let's convert some of those hardstandings into something a bit more diversity-encouraging and fecund.

Advice on creating your own wild garden, including choosing native tree and plant species for other regions can be obtained by the author's consultancy service. Contact Gerry at info@gerrymaguirethompson.com, or visit the website listed in the bibliography.

"There is a love of wild nature in everyone"

- John Muir, *early pioneer of the conservation movement*

Bibliography and online resources

Website for this book and garden: urbanwildgarden.com. Photos, video clips, blogs and latest news items about the garden can be found here.

Author website: gerrymaguirethompson.com

Wilding Isabella Tree - highly inspiring account of the journey toward rewilding the influential Knepp Estate in UK, and exploration of the issues involved

The Book of Wilding- Isabella Tree and Charlie Burrell

The Garden Jungle Dave Goulson - a comprehensive, fascinating and entertaining book about invertebrates in the garden, with practical measures you can take to support them

Deep Country Neil Ansell - a classic of nature writing wherein the author describes his experience of five years living totally isolated and off-grid in the remotest reaches of Wales, and his numerous extraordinary and intimate encounters with wildlife

The Wild Life: John Lewis Stempel - excellent description of the year the author spent living entirely on wild food, which proved challenging at times to say the least

Common Ground Rob Cowen - over a year the author discovers the wonders of what seems like local wasteland; also meshes with emotional elements of his own personal story

Still Water John Lewis Stempel - a fascinating, hugely informative and poetic exploration of the wildlife potential of ponds

Claxton Mark Cocker - Beautifully observed and detailed year-round chronicle of wildlife around the author's home village, by long-time nature and wildlife columnist

The House Sparrow- monograph, Denis Summersmith

Raptor - James Macdonald Lockhart

Entangled Life Merlin Sheldrake - an amazing analysis of how fungi underly absolutely all forms of life

Back to Nature Chris Packham and Megan McCubbin - how ordinary people can become activists and play a role in saving nature

Pilgrim at Tinker Creek Annie Dillard 1974 - a spell-binding account of local wildlife through the seasons; a bit trippy, but an influential nature book

The Snow Leopard Peter Matthiessen 1978 - a classic diarised account of a quest in search of wildlife in the high Himalayan mountains of Tibet and Nepal, together with an account of the personal and spiritual experience involved

A *Sand County Almanac* Aldo Leopold 1970 - one of the most influential wildlife/conservation books of the twentieth century, and a joy to read

Bill Bailey's Remarkable Guide to Happiness - by the top comedian, nature lover and conservationist

The Inside Out Revolution Michael Neill - proposes that the way we think about circumstances affects us more than the circumstances themselves

The Salt Path Raynor Winn - an inspiring book about the regenerative power of nature

Last Child in the Woods Richard Louv - an introduction to the concept of 'nature deficit disorder'

Rewilding an Urban Garden

Silent Spring Rachel Carson - the hugely influential wake-up call to the environmental dangers of chemicals used in the countryside

BBC TV: *Springwatch/ Autumnwatch/ Winterwatch:* Seminal tv series with in-depth coverage of wildlife through the seasons

BBC TV: Any output by David Attenborough (which started in 1951!) *eg Life on Earth, Life in the Undergrowth, and more recently the highly influential Extinction: the facts and A Perfect Planet*

My Octopus Teacher: 2020 film with Craig Foster - heart-achingly beautiful documentary about a diver's relationship with a wild octopus over the course of a year

ecowatch.com/birds-happiness-study-2649413979.html

- an academic study which quantifies the remarkable contribution that having birds around makes to your personal happiness

How to build an instant wild pond: urbanwildgarden.com/steps-to-create-an-instant-wild-pond-in-your-garden/

Acknowledgements

To Elaine Bellamy for life support.

To Mark Cocker, Neil Ansell, Fiona Robertson, Debbie Chapman, Jane Dumbrell, Magnus Sylven, Hazle Boyles, Tony Cooper, Paul Cowpertwait, and Andy Mindel for encouragement and practical help in developing manuscript and illustrations.

To Charlie Burrell and Issie Tree for inspiration.

To Ruth Stevens for sponsorship of illustrations.

To all the wild creatures, plant beings, fungal entities and bacteria for taking up home or spending quality time in our little garden.

To Marina for collaboration on the illustrations.

To Waheduzzaman Manik for book design and formatting.

Contact details:

Gerry Maguire Thompson
aka The Germinator™

gerrymaguirethompson.com
urbanwildgarden.com
info@gerrymaguirethompson.com
gerry@urbanwildgarden.com

+44 (0)7986 561 860
Chez di Nook BN43 5WL

The author would love to hear about your experiences with wild gardening and associated matters.

Also by the author:

Cats are from Venus, Dogs are from Mars

Astral Sex to Zen Teabags, a New Age Spoofapedia

Inspirational Gamechangers

Meditation Made Easy

The Celtic Oracle

The Shiatsu Manual

The Encyclopedia of the New Age

Printed in Great Britain
by Amazon

f020039d-400a-4972-b091-1905a5833bc7R01